A
Floral
Feast

CAROLYN DUNSTER

A Floral Feast

A guide to growing and cooking with edible flowers, foliage, herbs and seeds

Contents

Floral notes

There is no real evidence to determine when flowers were first used in cooking, but as long as people have been preparing and flavouring food we can assume they have been on the ingredients list. There is proof that in China cooks were experimenting with chive flowers in 3000 BC and that the Romans frequently added roses, violets and lavender to their menus. Age-old cookery manuals show recipes for blooms and flowering herbs that were incorporated into both sweet and savoury dishes for extra nourishment and embellishment.

Today, although many cultures still use flowers in traditional cooking, all too often they are seen as an exotic extra employed only by professional chefs in fine-dining restaurants and cookery shows on television. Whilst we are all taking a greater interest in the provenance of our food, adding more plant-based ingredients to our diets, experimenting with growing our own vegetables and eating to follow the seasons, edible flowers still remain a bit of an unknown quantity.

My aim in *A Floral Feast* is to introduce you to a whole range of ornamental flowers, herb and vegetable flowers, flower seeds and flower foliage that you can grow yourself for eating. Some of them taste delicious and are highly nutritious, whilst others are on the list purely because they are beautiful, easy to cultivate and will bring something new and exciting into the kitchen. They can turn an ordinary looking plate of food into one that is a feast for the eyes.

Growing flowers has been my personal and professional passion, and over many years my small city garden has been the test bed for my work. I don't have a huge plot and, first and foremost, I want a space that is lovely to look at, but I also want to be able to use my garden-grown flowers productively. To date, this has taken different forms and I've written widely about the best flowers to grow for picking and arranging and the ones I would recommend for cutting and drying.

Learning about edible flowers has taken me beyond the decorative aspects of flower

My plot-to-plate flowers have fuelled my creativity in the kitchen, and they elevate the run-of-the-mill family recipes that I make on repeat into something very special.

growing and appeals as a way of marrying two vital life forces: growing and eating. Experimenting with the use of flowers in food as an integral ingredient, a flavour enhancer or as an appetizing garnish has turned out to be a hugely satisfying gardening endeavour. Whilst I am not a professional chef my plot-to-plate flowers have fuelled my creativity in the kitchen, and they elevate the run-of-the-mill family recipes that I make on repeat into something very special.

The directory on page 120 is designed as an introductory guide to the wide number of garden flowers, also known as edimentals, that are safe to eat. You may already have some of them growing in your garden or you might like the idea of creating a designated edible flower patch as part of a wider kitchen garden. Many varieties can be grown in pots and containers for balcony or courtyard gardens, and if outdoor space is non-existent then scented pelargoniums are the perfect house plants. Cultivating your own edible flowers following organic principles means

that there is no danger of consuming anything that has been sprayed or treated. Never, under any circumstances, eat flowers bought from a florist shop. It is possible to source flowers for eating from specialist producers, but availability is often quite limited. Growing your own and avoiding the food miles is far more sustainable. Turn your gardening space into a pretty outdoor larder and you will reap the rewards on many fronts.

Creating an edible flower garden

There are many benefits to creating an edible flower garden. Firstly, I believe there is no question that flowers improve and enhance daily life, and there is nothing better than being able to pick a few blooms from outside your back door to use as a freshly picked garden-to-plate cooking ingredient. There is plenty of evidence to show that regular contact with nature is essential to our well-being and growing your own flowers and/or vegetables or observing them up-close in the wild can be an act of kindness to yourself and a way of connecting with the wider world.

Growing your own flowers from seed is pure magic and the best form of therapy, requiring no technical intervention or any complicated instruction. All that's needed are soil, light, water and patience (building reserves of the latter is no bad thing when instant gratification has become the norm). Being outside and getting your hands into the earth releases feel-good endorphins that improve mood and cognitive function. There is also some early scientific research indicating that healthy soil bacteria (*Mycobacterium vaccae*) on the skin and under our fingernails can interact positively with our gut bacteria and boost the immune system.

The nurturing of plants is deeply rooted in our DNA — it's what we have done for millennia to guarantee our survival. Our ancestors evolved from hunter-gatherers into farmers and gardeners tending plots of land, essentially to feed themselves and their animals, and learning at the same time how to interact and work with the soil and the seasons. Over time, most of us have lost those skills but it is imperative for our own mental health and the overall future of the planet that we regain them. Growing our own food gives us more control and helps to develop a stronger sense of agency over the way we can make a positive difference to our immediate surroundings. Despite a rural exodus during the COVID-19 pandemic, it is estimated that by 2050 80 per cent of the population in the United Kingdom will be living in a town or city. The same is true for other industrialized

*Growing your own flowers from seed is
pure magic and the best form of therapy,
requiring no technical intervention or
any complicated instruction.*

countries, but as more people choose to live in urban areas, wild green spaces where nature is currently left to flourish unchecked are increasingly being lost to development.

Make small changes

By making and tending gardens that are not too neat and manicured, letting go of the idea of a perfect but sterile green lawn and embracing 'weeds' (especially dandelions, which are delicious to eat), we can each make small changes that together have a much larger impact. City streets change dramatically when they are lined with trees and front gardens are filled with shrubs and vibrant flowers. Not only are they visually more pleasing than uniform blocks of hard landscaping, but plants are vital to the environment: they clean the air by absorbing pollution, they help to mitigate against climate change by cooling down the atmosphere in hot weather and they provide natural defences against flooding during heavy rainfall. Every garden, back yard and balcony packed

with plants becomes more than the sum of its parts, providing important corridors for wildlife in towns and cities and ensuring a green legacy for future generations.

Choosing to create an edible flower garden contributes hugely to this endeavour. A lot of the plants that bear flowers suitable for eating have similar recognizable characteristics: they tend to bear brightly coloured, single-headed blooms with a long flowering period and many of them are strongly perfumed. These happen to be the kind of flowers that attract bees, butterflies, moths, ladybirds, hoverflies and other pollinating insects. Eighty per cent of flowering plants rely on insects for pollination, which is the transfer of pollen from one flower to the stigma, or female reproductive organs, of another, resulting in fertilization and the formation of seeds and, eventually, new plants. Vibrant perfumed blooms have evolved specifically to attract pollinators and many species of flowers and insects have developed mutualistic relationships to ensure

Layering your planting at different heights and allowing plants to intermingle with no obvious stops and starts provides a sense of continuity and this is also the best way to increase the biodiversity of your space.

their individual and joint survival. This is known as coevolution — one species cannot exist without the other — and many flowers have adapted a wide variety of shapes and sizes to reflect the anatomy and habits of their insect counterparts. Put simply, if one dies out so does the other.

Plant to help wildlife

By growing lots of different types of edible ornamental flowers or creating a small edible flower patch within a larger garden, your growing space will immediately become a focus for a wide range of insects, which is the first step to establishing a well-balanced mini ecosystem. In turn the insects will attract birds and small mammals, so your garden becomes energized, busy with the buzzing of pollinators, the rustling of life in the leaves and the sound of birdsong. By welcoming as much wildlife as possible you are encouraging nature to take care of itself and carry out its own form of pest management. Gardening organically so that you can

safely eat your homegrown flowers means no spraying with any kind of pesticides or chemicals, but the birds, beetles and ladybirds will helpfully deal with the aphids and slugs.

To make a garden that is a welcome and safe place for wildlife and for people, there needs to be an underlying feeling of atmosphere or what is known as *genius loci*, commonly translated as 'the spirit of place'. This means creating a garden where there is a sense of flow that exudes calm and where nothing jars or feels uncomfortable. Visitors will immediately relax. It is difficult to devise a precise design formula for this, but in essence it is all about the planting. A green backdrop is crucial to blur the boundaries and create some seclusion unless you are surrounded by countryside. Growing plants in abundance provides a sense of generosity — encourage any prolific self-seeders to take the lead. If one type of flower performs particularly well, then repeat it in different hues so that you end up with fewer patches of bare soil and dense rich pockets of flowers to pick from.

Think about layers

Layering your planting at different heights and allowing plants to intermingle with no obvious stops and starts provides a sense of continuity. This is also the best way to increase the biodiversity of your space.

Start an upper storey with edible climbers for disguising walls and fences and, if you have room, plant a tree. A small fruit tree would be an obvious choice — all fruit blossoms can be eaten safely but you will also have the added advantage of enjoying the fruits later in the season if you don't consume all the blossom flowers. You can also eat the foliage of trees such as an olive or fig. Toast fig leaves in the oven and crumble them over salads or use olive leaves fresh or dried to make a tea rich in antioxidants and vitamin C.

The next level down would be some shrubs (see page 32 in A Guide to Flower Growing). Choose evergreen and deciduous shrubs that produce edible flowers but also provide cover and shelter for crawling insects and small birds. Perfumed shrubs such as roses will also contribute to a strong sense of atmosphere. It's possible to create an overlay of scent, particularly in a small garden, by combining different fragrant plants — the most useful when it comes to flavouring food — that have different growing habits and heights. Finally, decide which flowers — a mix of bulbs, perennials and annuals — you really want to grow, thinking about their textures and shapes, their flowering times and any other characteristics. Do they need full sun or partial shade? How water dependent are they? Make a list or draw up a simple plan of your growing area. To avoid expensive mistakes, work out which plants will thrive where before you begin and, when it comes to growing flowers for eating, choose the ones that seem most appealing in terms of taste. Whilst it is good to experiment there is no point growing fennel, for example, if you hate the taste of aniseed.

No-dig gardening

If you want to create an edible flower patch from scratch, then follow the no-dig method. Choose an area of flat ground — it could be part of a lawn — and cover it with thick brown cardboard in a square or rectangular shape. Recycled packaging boxes, with all tape removed, are perfect for this and will suppress any weeds or grass and act as a temporary base. They will gradually rot down over time. Cover the cardboard with a 10cm (4in) layer of organic peat-free compost and wait for two weeks. If it doesn't rain you will need to water the compost at least once to keep it moist. You can then plant directly into the compost — sow seeds or lay out plug plants in rows for easy access to picking. Full planting instructions are provided in A Guide to Flower Growing (see page 22) but it is important to state that a light touch is all that is required and there is no need to dig deep when creating new flower beds. Any turf or soil underneath the cardboard should remain undisturbed — this helps to retain the carbon

stored underground rather than releasing it into the atmosphere.

Healthy soil equals healthy plants. Soil contains mycorrhizal fungi that make up an intricate and delicate network that joins with the roots of plants as a way of transferring water, carbon, nitrogen and all the other nutrients and minerals a plant requires to thrive. It is a natural ecosystem that can look after itself but if it is continually disturbed by too much digging or depleted by flooding, the fertility of your soil will suffer. You can help by using an organic mulch in the gaps between your plants that enriches the soil as it breaks down. There is no need to dig it in as the worms will gradually do this job and the same goes for leaving leaf litter, fallen twigs and the remains of spent annual flowers to decompose on the surface. They serve as food for the soil beneath that will, in turn, nourish next year's flowers, making a perfect circle of sustainable and productive gardening practice with immediate benefits for now and for the future.

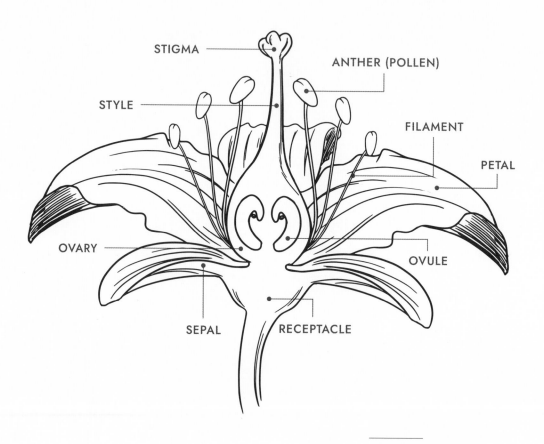

STIGMA + STYLE + OVARY = CARPEL

STIGMA

ANTHER (POLLEN)

STYLE

FILAMENT

PETAL

OVARY

OVULE

SEPAL

RECEPTACLE

FILAMENT + ANTHER = STAMEN

Anatomy of a flower

Flowers are composed of many distinct component parts, each one having their own unique function. For the purposes of eating flowers it is useful to understand what each part does.

Anther This is the male part of the flower where pollen is produced and is essential to a plant's reproductive life. It is not always visible, which is why you will sometimes see pollinating insects burying themselves deep inside a flower.

Calyx This is the collective name for the petal-like leaves also known as sepals at the base of a flower forming an outer protective layer when the flower is in bud. These should be removed before eating.

Carpel This is the collective name for the stigma, style and ovary.

Filament The main function of the filament is to carry nutrients to the anther for the development of pollen grains. It looks like a slender stalk.

Ovary This is the female reproductive organ of a flower. It contains an ovule that will develop into seeds if fertilized by pollen.

Ovule Once pollinated the ovule will swell as seeds start to form. Once seeds are mature they will disperse naturally to create new flowers.

Petal The main function of the petals is to attract pollinators. They tend to be the edible part of any flower. The white or yellow heel at the base of a petal can be bitter to taste and should be cut off before consumption.

Receptacle This keeps the flower in an elevated position, holding it upright so it will attract pollinating insects. It holds all the floral parts together.

Sepals These look like petals in appearance but tend to be green in colour (see calyx); these are not harmful if eaten but are generally bitter and tough.

Stamen This is the collective name for the anther and filament.

Stigma This is where the pollen germinates.

Style This is a tube-like structure that supports the stigma and connects it to the ovary.

A guide to flower growing

Growing your own flowers is incredibly satisfying and rewarding – growing them for cooking and eating is the horticultural cherry on the top. If you are a novice gardener, it is useful to know a little about the different types of flowers you decide to grow, and to understand their individual habits and what to expect from their performance. Although flower growing is not complicated it can be a little confusing and this chapter is designed to be used in conjunction with the edibles directory on page 120, so you can refer from one to the other for information.

Annual flowers

As their name indicates, annual flowers put all their energy into flowering in one season. Like a vegetable crop, they complete their whole life cycle from germination to harvest within one year or less. Once this has happened, any remaining flowers will set seed — this means the heads will gradually change and swell to form hard, protective seed pods which house the tiny beginnings of new flowers. It is a joy to watch this process take place on your plants and witness the miracle of nature that requires no human intervention whatsoever — it is exactly how most wild flowers reproduce. In a garden setting, you can collect this seed once it is mature — some of these seeds are edible (see page 160) but in all cases you can save it for resowing in designated positions or allow the seed pods to disperse naturally and produce new flowers in unexpected places. Having done its work, the parent plant will die back and not make any more flowers of its own.

The most efficient way to grow annuals is from a packet of seeds. If you are creating a new garden from scratch or you want to experiment with several different varieties, it is the most cost-effective way of growing lots of flowers. As they don't develop deep root systems many annuals thrive in pots and containers and tend to bloom more quickly as the soil in pots warms up faster. If you have the space, purpose-built raised beds make the best home for orderly rows of annuals grown kitchen-garden style for convenient picking. Alternatively, inserting some edible flowers into an existing border is easily done with small home-sown plants to fill the gaps.

Annuals are split into two types: hardy and half-hardy. This dictates the sowing time. Check the instructions on the seed packet so you know what you are dealing with. Edible hardy annuals such as sunflowers (*Helianthus annuus*), cornflowers (*Centaurea*) or pot marigolds (*Calendula*) will survive temperatures below freezing and can be sown directly into the ground in both autumn and spring. If it is very cold, a hardy annual

planted in the autumn will become dormant during the winter and start growing again in the spring. Half-hardy annuals including zinnias *(Zinnia)* (shown above) do not do this — they will die if they are exposed to very cold weather. If you decide to sow half-hardy seeds wait until any risk of frost has passed or start them off in a heated greenhouse or indoors on a windowsill.

Both hardy and half-hardy annuals can be sown successionally. This means dividing the seeds and sowing them at staged intervals of several weeks so you have flowers to pick over a long period.

ABOVE *Annuals make for easy edible pickings.*

Select a mix of edible hardy and half-hardy annuals for a floral harvest of up to six months of the year.

Seed sowing

Sowing your own seeds allows you to experiment to see what works and what doesn't in your own particular growing space at little cost. It also means you will most likely end up with excess plants that you can give away to friends or join in plant swaps.

Indoor seed sowing

Start the process of indoor sowing with a reusable seed tray or a suitable shallow, flat-bottomed, self-draining container. Fill your tray almost to the top with damp peat-free compost. Depending on the size of the seeds, sprinkle or use your fingers to poke the seed gently into the compost; tiny seeds should be sown sparingly, and larger seeds need to be spaced out. Remember to label them! Set the tray aside in a light place, ideally a window ledge. Seeds require warmth and light to germinate. Keep the compost damp by misting gently or sitting the bottom of the tray in water. Avoid using a watering can at this stage as the force of the water tends to wash the seed out of the compost.

Depending on the seeds, after 10–14 days you will see signs of germination as the seeds burst out of their coating. Tiny seedlings with pairs of dark green leaves will make their way through the compost to reach the light. These first leaves are false and known as cotyledons but are integral to the plant's growth. Soon after, the seedlings will form their first true leaves, which have the appearance and function that all future leaves will have – they may look dramatically different to the cotyledons.

Once you see at least one set of true leaves and the seedlings have grown a little height they need to acclimatize or 'harden off'. On a warm day put the tray outside but bring it in again at night. As they put on further growth, they will need more space and depth – your seedlings need to be 'pricked out'. This means they should be transferred to their own individual pots. Biodegradable coir pots are ideal. Fill with compost and make a hole with your finger or a blunt pencil. Use a knife or a teaspoon to scoop each seedling from

the bottom of the seed tray without damaging its fragile roots. Hold it by its true leaves and place securely so the roots are in the new hole, firming them in with the surrounding compost. Your seedlings are now ready to move outside. Water regularly and keep a close check on their development. Once the coir pot is full of bushy green growth you can plant it into the ground or put several pots into a large container. The roots will grow through the coir pots, which will decompose naturally.

Outdoor seed sowing

If you want to skip the above stages for indoor seed sowing, follow instructions on the seed packets for sowing or broadcasting directly where you want them to grow. Your seedlings will germinate in the same way. Once you see the false leaves appear you need to 'thin out' the seedlings. Select the seedling with the sturdiest set of leaves and remove all the others surrounding it. This gives one plant the greatest chance of survival and will allow it the space it needs to put on further growth.

ABOVE *Start seeds off in pots and watch them germinate.*

Perennial flowers

Perennials are flowering plants that live for several years. Many perennials produce edible flowers that come back reliably every season from the same parent. They are generally divided into two groups: short-lived – up to about three years – or long-lived – five years or more. They are also divided into two categories: tender and hardy. A tender perennial such as an African daisy (Osteospermum) will not survive temperatures below freezing and will need protection from the cold. These are best grown in pots so that they can be moved inside or into a greenhouse during the winter. Hardy perennials like peonies (Paeonia) and flowering sages (Salvia) will die back above ground in the winter, but their roots will continue to grow underground. Both the roots and the top growth of perennials spread over time and the plants gradually get bigger and bigger. If you are growing them in pots, they are likely to need repotting yearly as their roots expand and they need more space.

Propagating from division

By lifting and dividing hardy perennials growing in the ground you can keep plants to a manageable size and rejuvenate them. This is generally done in the autumn when flowering has finished and it is a way to create a stock of new plants for free. Dig up the whole plant and simply pull apart at the roots, or be brave and cut through with a serrated knife. Pot up each rooted piece separately in a container or plant back into the ground in a different area.

Propagating from cuttings

Another way to create new plants from perennials is to take softwood cuttings from a parent plant. Tender perennials such as pelargoniums will produce bushy shoots on a main stem that can be cut off at a mid-point before the next set of leaves form. Insert the cutting into fresh compost in a new pot until roots form and you can see fresh top growth appearing. This is an inexpensive way of propagating plants.

Other ways to grow perennials

There are several ways to start growing perennials depending on how much space you have, how much money you want to spend and how patient you are prepared to be. You can grow them from seed in the same way as annuals, but they may not flower profusely until their second year. You can purchase mature plants that will flower straight away and provide you with instant material for dividing or you can buy pre-grown seedlings and plug plants from nurseries at the beginning of the growing season. These offer the best compromise — someone else has done the fiddly work and all you need to do is plant them in the ground or in a container.

ABOVE *Small perennials such as* dianthus *and* osteospermum *grow well in pots.*

29

Bulbs and tubers

Many edible flowers grow from bulbs. The most obvious are onion flowers and this is a good example of how a bulb performs. If left uneaten, an onion will eventually start to sprout green shoots of its own accord, which is what all bulbs do when planted in soil. Bulbs are essentially mini, individual storage units made up of fibrous fleshy material with a growing point at their centre. You can see this when you slice an onion in half.

Although mostly associated with spring, there are many different bulbs that produce flowers for eating throughout the year. They vary greatly in shape and size — generally the larger the bulb the larger the flower head, and this provides a clue as to how and where to plant them. You can cram lots of tiny grape hyacinth (*Muscari*) bulbs into a pot for example, and the same goes for tulips *(Tulipa)*. Although they are bigger they have no objection to being planted quite close together and this is the way to get the best display. You can also layer bulbs in pots to create a bulb 'lasagna', with larger bulbs

at the bottom and smaller ones near the top and compost in between. If you plant them in borders or in wide open spaces they will 'naturalize', meaning they will multiply and spread themselves around to form new plants that you can eventually dig up to fill gaps elsewhere. To allow them to do this resist cutting any foliage back after flowering. The leaves are essential for capturing sunlight to recharge the bulb and create energy for producing flowers the following year.

Plan seasonal planting

If you are planting bulbs for the first time then some planning ahead is required. Spring and early summer flowering bulbs should be planted in the previous autumn and early winter. They require a period of cold in the ground to activate the biochemical process that encourages them to flower. Late summer and autumn flowering bulbs should be planted in spring. Follow the planting instructions provided on the bulb pack — as a rule of thumb, bulbs should be planted into

soil at twice their depth and with the nose or pointed end facing upwards.

Planting corms, rhizomes and tubers

Although different in appearance and structure to bulbs, corms, rhizomes and tubers have the same overall planting requirements. Some have particular needs that become apparent once you start to grow them. Dahlias (*Dahlia),* which are delicious to eat and so beautiful to look at, grow from tubers that do not survive for long in freezing ground. Depending on your location, they may need to be lifted and stored somewhere cool and dry for replanting in the spring. It is time consuming but well worth the effort.

Plant tulips and dahlias for an edible flower harvest in spring and autumn and extend the growing season.

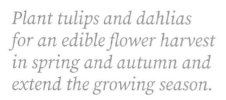

ABOVE *Begonias and alliums grow from small bulbs.*

31

Shrubs and climbers

Shrubs and climbers are integral to any garden. From a design point of view, they create permanent structures and shapes that form the backbone to any successful planting scheme, especially if it is based on growing lots of annual and perennial flowers that disappear in the winter months. However, their greater benefit is environmental — as every single plant has its own specific ecosystem, the wider the variety of plants in any growing space the greater the overall biodiversity. You will attract more insects, birds and other wildlife if you can provide them with a varied but constant supply of food and places to shelter. In turn they will pollinate your flowers and distribute their seeds.

Shrubs

Edible flowering shrubs such as lilac (Syringa), elderflower (Sambucus) and roses (Rosa) are deciduous, meaning that they lose their leaves in winter but they still look good when stripped back to their bare bones. Do not be too quick to clear away fallen foliage as this provides a home for hibernating insects, material for birds' nests and nutrients for your soil. Let the worms do their job and don't worry about keeping your garden too tidy. Other edible flowering shrubs such as camellias (Camellia) keep their leaves once their flowers have gone over to provide permanent year-round interest.

Planting in containers

You can grow shrubs in pots or plant them in the ground. Pots will need to be upsized every few years but regular trimming will prevent the roots from expanding too quickly. They will also need more frequent watering as roots in pots dry out more quickly. A thorough drenching once a week is more efficient than a daily spray and sitting your pot on a large saucer is the best way to capture excess drainage. If a potted plant has completely dried out, then stand it in a bucket of water for a few hours.

Climbers

Jasmine *(Jasminium)*, passion vine *(Passiflora)* and honeysuckle *(Lonicera)* are all climbing plants that produce edible flowers. Climbers are the perfect boundary plants that help to create a natural sense of privacy and seclusion, especially in a small, terraced garden that is overlooked on all sides. Wherever you have a bare wall or a fence cover it with climbers. They will need some initial artificial support via a trellis or wires to provide a basic framework but once established they will continue to grow upwards following the light. When planting against a wall, position individual plants approximately 25–30cm (10–12in) away from the wall and angle them towards it. If you plant too close to the concrete foundations the roots will never get enough moisture.

GROWING FLOWERS FOR EATING

The Royal Horticultural Society (RHS) recommends that if you are purchasing flowering plants to grow for eating from a non-organic nursery or supplier it is advisable to wait for at least three months before harvesting any flowers. Do not eat any flowers that initially arrive on the plant. After three months of growing in your own garden any risk of pesticide residues from the original growing medium will have disappeared.

For more information visit rhs.org.uk/ herbs/edible-flowers

ABOVE *No garden, however small, is complete without an edible climbing rose.*

Grow your own

This chapter shines the spotlight on ten key flowering plants that are a feast for both the eyes and the palate. They form the mainstay of my own edible flower garden and include a mix of annuals and perennials, shrubs and climbers. For those without an outdoor growing space marigolds, pinks, fennel, nasturtiums, sunflowers and lavender will all grow happily in pots on a balcony or wide window ledge, whilst pelargoniums can be treated as house plants. I have adapted the accompanying recipes to maximize the flavour and beauty of each given plant, but they can be easily reconfigured to use other flowers of a similar habit.

Calendula
Pot marigold, common marigold, English marigold

A hardy annual with edible petals and leaves

HEIGHT & SPREAD 50 x 50cm (20 x 20in)

The cheerful daisy-like flowers of marigolds bring pops of joy to any growing space and can be used in multiple dishes to bring your food to life. As hardy annuals they are extremely easy to grow – simply divide a packet of seeds and sow half in the autumn and the remainder in the spring by scattering directly on to the ground. You will have flowers to pick throughout the summer and beyond. *Calendula* also performs well in small pots and containers as the roots remain shallow.

To keep plants compact and bushy, pinch out the top shoots to promote growth in the form of side shoots further down the main stem. Regular picking of the flowers will encourage more to come. If you notice that they have started to form seed heads early in the season, cut them off as they will prevent further flowering. At the end of the summer, you can remove and save some seed heads for resowing or simply leave on the plant. The seed will set *in situ* and then disperse naturally to make new plants in unexpected places.

There are many varieties ranging from peachy pink hues to buttery yellows but the one I like to use best in cooking is 'Indian Prince'. It's a rich burnt orange that imparts the best colour. Harvest the flowers once they are fully open. You can use them fresh or dry. If using fresh, then gently remove the petals from the main flower head and store in the fridge in a sealed container. If drying, place the heads upside down on a flat board and keep somewhere warm away from direct light. Within a week the flowers will have dried. Remove the petals and transfer to a jar. They will keep for several months without losing their colour. At this stage you can grind them with a pestle and mortar to make your own calendula powder.

Calendula works like saffron in cooking and will tint and subtly flavour a variety of foods. You can use it generously in soups, stews, casseroles and rice-based dishes, and sparingly in baking and desserts. It makes a wonderful natural colourant for icing. The flavour is best described as zesty with a hint of grassiness. The leaves are very aromatic with a peppery taste and can be picked to use in salads – complement with a scattering of fresh petals to liven things up.

CALENDULA RISOTTO

1   Set a pan on a low heat and add the olive oil.

2   Add the diced shallots and garlic and cook gently until softened.

3   Stir in the rice and mix well until every grain is coated in oil.

4   Pour in 60ml (4 tbsp) white wine until it has evaporated, and continue adding the rest of the wine in increments.

5   Add the stock to the rice, a ladle at a time, waiting until all the liquid has been absorbed before adding more.

6   Add the dried calendula flowers with the final ladle of stock and stir in gently for an even distribution.

7   Your risotto is cooked when the rice is soft and unctuous and all the liquid has been absorbed — you will need to test it.

8   Transfer to a serving bowl and scatter the fresh calendula petals over the top.

9   Serve with a flower or green leaf salad.

Serves 6

45ml (3 tbsp) olive oil
1500ml (3 pints) calendula stock (see recipe on page 101)
2 shallots, finely chopped
4 garlic cloves, finely chopped
400g (3¾ cups) arborio rice
160ml (6 fl oz) white wine
3 handfuls of dried calendula petals (see page 37)
1 handful of fresh calendula petals

Dianthus
Pink, carnation, sweet william

A hardy perennial with edible petals

HEIGHT & SPREAD 30 x 20cm (12 x 8in)

Pinks and carnations have been cultivated as ornamental garden plants since the Middle Ages. They are native to Asia and certain parts of southern Europe where *Dianthus carthusianorum* can be spotted growing in the wild in dry grassy habitats. They are literally known as the 'flowers of the gods' — *Dios* derives from the Greek meaning 'of Zeus' and *anthos* means flower. For this reason, they have historically been regarded as highly symbolic flowers with spiritual connotations. In medieval times they featured widely as popular decorative motifs. In recent years they have fallen from grace but they are poised to make a big comeback.

New introductions such as 'Tequila Sunrise', 'Sugar Plum' and 'Coconut Sundae' hint at why they should be a key plant in an edible flower garden. Their intense sweet/spicy clove-like scent is indicative of their taste and they are a delicious addition to all kinds of recipes. Turn them into sugars for cakes and biscuits or add to ice creams and sorbets. The frilly, brightly coloured petals, often trimmed with a two-tone edging, look fabulous floating in drinks or scattered as food confetti over finished dishes just before serving. Be sure to cut off the white heel at the base beforehand as this has a bitter aftertaste.

Pinks and carnations are part of the same family and both are edible, but there are some significant differences: pinks are smaller and hardier and like to be outside whereas carnations grow taller, are generally fussier and should be well protected, ideally under glass. Grow both from seed started indoors in the very early spring or buy small plants in early summer. Pinks can be transferred to a border or cutting patch. Plant them in a sunny spot right at the front for the best display. They will form small cushions of foliage from which the flowers grow upright on strong straight stems. Regular picking will keep them compact and they are an ideal plant for a small space. For small pots look out for miniature alpine varieties. They require well-drained soil and do not like to become waterlogged. Adding some horticultural grit will provide extra drainage.

Dianthus is easy to propagate: cut off new green side shoots before they flower and place in a vase of cold water until you see some new roots form before potting up. Alternatively, plant cuttings directly into a seed tray of compost and cover with grit. This is the best way to create lots of free new plants for the following year.

DIANTHUS BLINIS WITH DIANTHUS-INFUSED HONEY

Blinis

1   Place all the dry ingredients in a mixing bowl and make a small well in the bottom.

2   Add the egg, melted butter and milk and beat by hand until everything is combined into a smooth batter.

3   Gently stir in half the dianthus petals so they are well distributed.

4   Put a small frying pan on the heat and add the extra butter.

5   When the butter has melted add a spoonful of batter so that it forms a small circle. I use a round metal cookie cutter to contain the batter and make the blinis one at a time.

6   As the blini starts to cook, sprinkle on a few more petals.

7   Once it is bubbling, release the blini from the cookie cutter and turn over to finish cooking, adding a few more petals.

8   Once the blini is cooked on both sides, transfer to a plate and follow the same procedure until you have used up the batter.

9   Stack them in a pile and drizzle the honey over the top.

10 Scatter with any leftover petals.

Honey

1   Tip the jar of honey into a small jug.

2   Place a layer of dianthus petals in the bottom of the original jar and pour a small amount of honey back in.

3   Add another layer of petals and repeat with the poured honey until you have filled the jar back up.

4   Finish with a layer of petals on top and seal with the original jar lid. It will keep for six months.

Makes about 8 small blinis

Blinis
110g (1⅛ cup) plain
    flour
½ tbsp baking powder
½ tsp sugar
Pinch of salt
1 beaten egg
30g (¼ stick) melted
    butter plus some
    for frying
150ml (5fl oz) milk
1–2 handfuls of fresh
    dianthus petals

Honey
1 small jar clear
    runny honey
1 small handful of
    fresh dianthus petals
    – mixed colours
    if possible

Foeniculum vulgare
Common fennel

A hardy perennial with edible flowers, foliage and seeds

HEIGHT & SPREAD 1.5m x 45cm (5ft x 18in)

Fennel thrives in any situation: it is undemanding, requires little maintenance and adapts very well to drought conditions. It is fast becoming a key plant to mitigate against climate change, and its usefulness in the kitchen means we should all be growing it. Seeds planted in the autumn or spring produce airy florets of bright yellow hues that hover above stems of feathery green foliage. Appearing continuously from mid- to late summer, the flowers are heavy in pollen and act as a magnet for bees and other insects. Their flat-topped heads make the perfect landing pad.

In autumn or spring scatter the seed where you want it to grow. Once you have seedlings of about 10cm (4in) high, thin them out so that your plants sit half a metre (20in) apart as the roots need plenty of space underground. Fennel grows to over a metre (4–5ft) high and creates a stunning structural silhouette against a wall or fence.

Native to the Mediterranean, large clumps of wild fennel *(Foeniculum sativus)* are a familiar sight in southern Europe where it is used widely in cooking. All parts including the stems and stalks are edible and have a mild aniseed flavour reminiscent of liquorice. Snip off individual florets to add a pop of colour to salads and cold vegetable dishes and use the leaves and stems in stews and soups or eat raw.

Once the flowers go over and seed heads start to form, cut off the stems with the heads intact, leaving a few short leaves at the base of the plant — it will come back the following year. As they ripen, the tiny individual seeds will detach themselves when the heads are gently shaken. Store them in an airtight jar to use in curries and for adding to pickles and preserves. In India the seeds are known as *saunf* and are renowned as a digestive aid. A handful chewed after a meal helps with digestion and freshens the mouth. Alternatively, make a soothing tisane by pouring boiling water over a few seeds and strain before drinking.

If you want to grow fennel bulbs for eating, then Florence fennel *(Foeniculum vulgare* var. *azoricum)* is the variety to look out for. It is trickier to cultivate and only yields one bulb per plant. I find it easier to buy bulbs from the farmers' market and dress with my homegrown flowers and foliage.

SHAVED FENNEL SALAD DRESSED WITH PICKLED FENNEL FLOWERS

Pickled flowers

1 Put the vinegar, sugar, half the fennel seeds and peppercorns in a saucepan. Place on a medium heat and stir until the sugar has dissolved.

2 Bring to a simmer for about two minutes.

3 Remove and allow to cool.

4 Place the fennel fronds and diced stalks in a sterilized (see page 80) 300ml (10fl oz) jar.

5 Gently cut the individual fennel florets from the flowers, using a pair of clean nail scissors, and add these to the jar.

6 Strain the cooled pickling liquid through a fine sieve or tea strainer over the contents of the jar and seal.

7 Keep the pickle refrigerated for at least two hours before use. It will keep for several weeks and can be added to soups and stews as well as salad dressings.

Salad

1 Remove and discard the tougher outer layer of the fennel bulb. With a very sharp knife, shave thin slivers from the remaining bulb on the diagonal and arrange on a plate.

2 Squeeze the juice from the lemon over the fennel to prevent it from turning brown.

3 Add some fronds and diced stalks to the plate and drizzle with the olive oil.

4 Spoon the pickled fennel flowers, some pickled fronds and stalks over the salad.

5 Sprinkle on the remaining fennel seeds.

6 Serve with plainly grilled chicken or fish or as an accompaniment to a cheese platter with crusty bread to mop up the pickle juices.

Serves 2

Pickled fennel flowers
300ml (10 fl oz) white wine vinegar
50g (⅓ cup) caster sugar
1 tsp fennel seeds
½ tsp black peppercorns
Small bunch of fennel fronds
Handful of diced fennel stalks
5 fennel flowers

Salad
I small fennel bulb, a few fennel fronds and stalks
Half a lemon
1 tbsp olive oil

Hibiscus syriacus
Rose of Sharon

A perennial shrub with edible petals

HEIGHT & SPREAD 2.5 x 4m (8 x 13ft)

Hibiscus is a group of flowering shrubs that are part of the larger mallow (*Malvaceae*) family. The flowers from this group tend to be wide and trumpet-shaped and act as an open larder for bees and other pollinating insects. They are easily recognized by the large, protruding stamen at their centre.

As their Latin name suggests, these plants were originally cultivated in the Middle East but they are hardy enough to survive northern winters outside.

To encourage their bushy habit they require some light pruning in the spring. Purchase from a nursery or garden centre as a small specimen and they will soon put on plenty of growth. Plant in full sun in well-drained soil, water well and they will reward you with a display of colour from mid- to late summer through until the autumn.

Hibiscus flowers open and close with the sun — as the daily temperature warms up, the tightly furled petals will open to reveal the full flower only to shut tight again in the evening. To harvest the flowers cut them in the middle of the day when they are in full bloom with a sharp pair of scissors or flower snips. Do not try and pick them by hand. They are very fragile and will bruise easily. Carefully separate the petals from the calyx — the green part at the centre of the flower — and discard the stamen (see page 18). Lay your petals out to dry and then store in an airtight container until you are ready to use them.

They have an intense fruity flavour reminiscent of blackcurrants mixed with plums. The petals contain vitamin C and are high in antioxidants. For this reason, they are revered in the practice of Ayurveda in India and in Chinese medicine for their therapeutic qualities. Dark pink or red varieties such as 'Flower Tower Ruby' make the best coloured juices and syrups.

HIBISCUS POACHED PEARS

1 Put the hibiscus juice and sugar in a saucepan large enough to accommodate the pears sitting side by side.

2 Bring to a boil, allow the sugar to dissolve and then reduce to a simmer.

3 Whilst this is happening peel each pear, leaving the stalk intact, and immediately transfer to the pan in turn so there is no time for the flesh to turn brown.

4 Baste each pear once with the sweetened hibiscus juice whilst it is in the pan ensuring a good coating.

5 Cover the pan with a lid and continue to simmer, spooning the hibiscus juice over the pears from time to time so they stay covered.

6 After 45 minutes turn the pears over – the pears will gradually take on the colour and flavour of the hibiscus juice. You are aiming for an even distribution of colour so continue to baste the pears with the juice for another 45 minutes or until they are soft.

7 Remove from the heat and allow to cool.

8 Transfer the pears to a separate plate or bowl.

9 Put the hibiscus juice back on the heat and bring to the boil. Continue to boil until it thickens to a syrup-like consistency.

10 Remove from the heat and immediately add a couple of spoonfuls to four individual serving dishes.

11 Handle your cooled pears very gently by the stalk and sit them upright in the syrup.

12 Allow to cool and when your pears are sitting very firmly spoon over the remaining syrup for a beautiful, glossy, garnet-coloured finish.

13 Serve with hibiscus granita (see page 95 in Culinary Extras).

Makes 4

4 large pears – just ripe but still firm to the touch
1000ml (2 pints) hibiscus juice (see page 88 in Culinary Extras)
100g (½ cup) caster sugar

Jasminium officinale
Common white jasmine

A perennial climber with edible flowers

HEIGHT & SPREAD 8 x 5.5m (26 x 18ft)

Whilst most commonly recognized as a flavouring for tea, the scented flowers of white jasmine have many further uses in cooking. Note that although the yellow flowers of winter jasmine are also edible and look pretty as a garnish, they have no discernible fragrance or flavour. The tiny star-shaped blooms of white jasmine, however, pack a strongly perfumed punch and put on a delightful show all summer long.

Jasmine is the perfect boundary plant for an edible flower garden. It quickly scrambles on a trellis or along wire runners to cover a wall or fence. As a deciduous plant it loses its leaves in autumn, but you will still be left with an attractive framework of stems to look at. You can train it to grow up a tree if no other space is available. Plant small specimens in spring or autumn and it will soon romp away. For a profusion of perfumed flowers, it needs direct sunlight — the oils in the flowers which produce the perfume and flavour are activated by heat.

Prune jasmine after flowering has finished. Cut back any damaged or unwieldy stems. If space is limited cut off any extraneous growth to keep it in check. You can be as tough as necessary, and it won't mind. New green shoots will appear at the base the following year. Water once after planting and then leave it to do its own thing — jasmine copes very well with dry conditions.

Pick individual flower heads as they appear. Store them in a sealed container in the fridge for batch-making jams or jellies. You will only need a few jasmine flowers to flavour individual dishes. Their sweet, slightly musky taste adds a floral note to cakes, desserts and puddings or add to rice and noodle dishes for a hint of fragrance. To make your own jasmine tea, layer fresh or dried flowers between black or green tea leaves, steep in boiling water and strain before drinking. There is evidence to suggest that the aroma has a calming effect on the nervous system and is a natural mood enhancer.

JASMINE NOODLE SALAD

1   Cook the noodles according to the instructions on the packet, drain and allow to cool. Toss them in the sesame oil to prevent them from congealing.

2   Prepare your vegetables and keep in separate piles.

3   Assemble your salad on a plate or in a shallow bowl starting with the noodles, and add in the vegetables aiming for an even distribution.

4   Mix the dressing ingredients in a small jug and pour over the salad.

5   Scatter over the nigella seeds.

6   Add the jasmine flowers just before serving.

Makes a large salad for one as a main course or two side salads

Salad
1 portion wholewheat
    noodles
¼ red pepper, cut
    into matchsticks
1 small carrot, grated
Small portion of
    cooked edamame
    beans or garden
    peas
Small portion of
    wakame seaweed
    or ¼ raw courgette,
    grated
1 spring onion, cut
    into rounds
10–15 fresh jasmine
    flowers
1 tsp sesame oil

Dressing
1 tsp lemon juice
1 tbsp jasmine water
    (see page 88 in
    Culinary Extras)
1 tbsp sesame oil
2 tsp nigella seeds

Lavandula
Lavender

A hardy perennial with edible flowers

HEIGHT & SPREAD 60 x 75cm (24 x 30in)

Lavender is best known for its therapeutic qualities and its distinctive perfume is very familiar. It is also available as a commercially produced food flavouring and you can find it in the baking aisles of most supermarkets. Lavender has a potent taste and should be used sparingly in cooking. If you use garden-grown flowers to make your own concoctions, you can adjust the flavour to suit your palate. Combine with lemon juice or other sharp-tasting juices such as cherry or blackcurrant for the perfect blend of floral and fruity.

All varieties of lavender flowers are edible and if you grow a range of plants you can easily extend their flowering season. Start with some French lavenders, which are the earliest to bloom at the beginning of summer, and follow through with some English varieties that flower until early autumn. One of my favourite lavenders to grow and use in cooking is *Lavendula angustifolia* 'Hidcote'. This is a compact form of English lavender which is perfect for lining a path or a border or the edge of a cut flower patch. Its deep violet flower spikes are intensely perfumed and contrast beautifully with its silvery-grey foliage. Clip to keep it in neat mounds for a formal contemporary setting or let it go a bit wild for a more naturalistic planting scheme. Either way, like all other lavenders, it will bring life to your garden with the continuous buzzing of all the insects it attracts.

Lavenders like to be baked in full sun. Plant them at any time as small specimens and they will soon put on lots of vigorous growth. They are happiest in well-drained soil and thrive in stony situations, making them ideal plants for a gravel garden. They hate to sit in the wet and require only minimal watering. Cut off any spent stems after flowering has finished and trim back to the first part of the green growth. This will encourage prolific flowering the following year. Avoid cutting into any brown wood as this will cause the plant to die.

You can harvest your lavender flowers at different stages of flowering. Detach the tiny florets from the main head when they are in full bloom to dress cakes and desserts. Do this gently with your fingers or a pair of tweezers. Use the whole flower heads to make syrups and cordials of an intense violet colour for cocktails. As the blooms start to fade pick bunches for drying. Hang them upside down in a warm space away from direct sunlight and once dry roll between your finger and thumb so the flower nibs come away from the head. Store in a glass jar for use over the winter to make sugars, jams and jellies.

LAVENDER & LEMON 'FROYO' WITH LAVENDER SHORTBREAD

Shortbread biscuits

1 Preheat the oven to 150°C/300°F/Gas Mark 2.

2 Cream together the butter and sugar.

3 Add in the flour and lavender flowers if not using lavender sugar, and combine first with a spoon and then with your hands to form a soft ball.

4 Transfer to a lightly floured work surface and roll out to ½cm/ ¼in thick.

5 Use a small heart- or round-shaped cookie cutter to cut out your biscuits.

6 Place biscuits on a greased baking sheet and cook for 30 minutes.

7 Sprinkle with a dusting of caster sugar as soon as they are removed from the oven.

8 Cool on a wire rack and store in an airtight tin. They will keep for several days.

Frozen yoghurt

1 Combine the yoghurt, lemon juice, lemon zest and lavender flowers.

2 Transfer to the original yogurt container, seal and freeze for at least two hours.

3 Allow to soften slightly before serving.

4 Scoop into individual serving bowls and drizzle with lavender syrup.

5 Dress with frosted lavender stems.

Makes 12–14

Shortbread biscuits
150g (1¼ sticks) cold butter cut into small pieces
80g (½ cup) caster sugar or lavender sugar (see page 92 in Culinary Extras)
200g (2 cups) plain flour
Handful of fresh individual lavender florets or 1 tbsp dried lavender

Frozen yoghurt
I large tub of Greek-style yogurt or dairy-free equivalent
Juice and zest of 1 unwaxed lemon
100ml (3fl oz) of lavender syrup (see page 79 in Culinary Extras)
Small handful of fresh individual lavender flowers or 1 tsbp of dried lavender
12 stems frosted lavender (optional, see page 84 in Culinary Extras)

Pelargonium
Storksbill

A tender perennial with edible foliage

HEIGHT & SPREAD 40 x 30cm (16 x 12in)

Pelargoniums are members of a family of plants known as *Geraniaceae*. Geraniums are widely grown garden plants native to the northern hemisphere and pelargoniums are often grouped together with them. It is their long beak-like seedheads that reflect the familial relationship: pelargoniums are commonly known as storksbills *(pelargos* being the ancient Greek name for stork) and geraniums are known as cranesbills *(gernos* is the ancient Greek for crane). For the purposes of growing pelargoniums as edible plants it is important not to confuse them with geraniums.

Pelargoniums are perennial plants that originally come from South Africa and will not tolerate frost. If you plant them in pots or containers they can easily be brought inside to sit on a windowsill during the colder months where you can enjoy them as house plants. Growing several different types of pelargoniums for their strongly perfumed foliage provides plenty of different options for flavouring food. Choose varieties such as 'Attar of Roses', 'Lemon Kiss' or 'Chocolate Peppermint' to use in different recipes. You will want to build up a collection and it is worth visiting a specialist grower before making your selection to determine your favourites.

Pelargoniums are easy to grow but they hate to have damp roots so consider adding some grit, gravel or vermiculite to improve drainage. From May to October you can grow your pelargoniums outside. Site them in a sunny spot and watch them put on regular bushy growth that will provide you with plenty of foliage for cutting. Water the roots little but often. When you bring them indoors for the winter you need only water once every few weeks to allow them to dry out. In autumn they need to have their foliage reduced and this is the time to remove a lot of leaves to make scented syrups to use throughout the winter. The plant needs air and light to reach all its parts to keep it healthy as it goes into dormancy. Cut back just above a leaf node with clean sharp scissors. Also remember to take off any yellowing or dead leaves as you see them to prevent disease. If at any time your plant looks like it is sickening, it is probably because it has been overwatered and/or because it is not getting enough light. This can be easily remedied by moving the plant to another position and holding back with the watering can.

PELLIE LOAF CAKE WITH PELLIE FROSTED TOPPING

Cake

1 Preheat the oven to 180°C/350°F/Gas Mark 4.

2 Oil and line a 450g (16oz) loaf tin with parchment paper.

3 Cream together the butter and pelargonium sugar. You can do this by hand or with electric beaters.

4 Add the eggs one at a time.

5 Mix the flour and ground almonds together and gradually fold into the batter.

6 Pour into the loaf tin.

7 Cook for about an hour — keep checking after 45 minutes and, if necessary, cover the top with foil so it doesn't burn. Test by inserting a skewer and wait until it comes out clean.

8 Allow your cake to cool completely before removing from the tin.

Topping

1 Mix the icing sugar and pellie water in a small jug, adding the liquid in increments until it starts to thicken but can still be poured evenly over the cake. Leave to drip down the sides.

2 Scatter with the shredded pelargonium leaves and sprinkle over the extra teaspoon of pellie sugar before the frosting sets.

Cake

150g (1½ sticks) butter
150g (¾ cup) pelargonium sugar plus an extra teaspoon (see page 92 in Culinary Extras)
3 eggs
125g (1 cup) self-raising flour
75g (¾ cup) ground almonds

Topping

70g (½ cup) icing sugar
3 tsp pelargonium water (see page 88 in Culinary Extras)
10 pelargonium leaves shredded into tiny pieces

Rosa
Rose

A shrub with edible flowers and petals

HEIGHT & SPREAD depends on the variety

Roses have been tried and tested as recipe ingredients for centuries. Rose-based food flavourings are easy to find if you want to buy them but for the most part, like cheap perfumes, they are synthetically produced, and the taste tends to be one dimensional. It is only by growing your own roses that you will discover the wide variety of rose fragrances. These range from spicy to sweet to fruity and create natural floral layers for more subtle and delicate uses in cookery.

No edible flower garden, however small, is complete without at least one scented rose: choose from a fragrant climber, a rambler, a shrub rose, a tea rose, a species or wild rose to fit your space. Look for those that flower repeatedly. Once established they need little care other than some pruning in late autumn or early spring. Roses prefer some sun but there are several varieties that will grow in shade such as 'Eustacia Vye' or 'Phyllis Bide' and there are many that grow happily in pots and containers – 'Noisette Blush' is one of the best. If you intend to use the petals for decoration, then the bright pink flowers of 'Gertrude Jekyll' and the velvety clarets of 'Munstead Wood' and 'Darcy Bussell' all retain their colour and hold up well to drying and crystallization.

There is rarely a rose that fails to thrive if it is correctly planted in the right place – ideally seek advice from a specialist rose nursery before buying. You can plant roses supplied as 'bare root' in the autumn when they will have no flowers or foliage and are wrapped in paper (soak the roots for at least two hours before planting), or wait until spring and purchase in a pot ready to transfer into a container or directly into the ground. Add some mycorrhizal fungi to the planting hole and ensure that the graft union, which is the bump at the base of the main stem, is at soil level and not buried. If you develop problems with white or black fly then wipe them away with a damp cloth. Remember, if you are going to eat your roses it is important not to spray with any chemicals. If you see black spot or rust on any leaves then cut them off immediately.

Harvest your roses as you would for flower arranging. Regular picking and deadheading encourages new growth. Use the petals, buds or whole flower heads fresh or dried for garnishes and decoration or make your own syrups, waters and cordials for flavouring drinks and a range of sweet and savoury dishes.

ROSE PAVLOVA

Meringue base

1 Preheat the oven to 130°C/220°F/Gas Mark 2.

2 Beat the egg whites until they start to form soft peaks.

3 Add the sugar, spoon by spoon, whilst continuing to beat.

4 Fold in the rose water.

5 Line a baking sheet with greaseproof paper. Draw round a medium-sized dinner plate on the paper so you have a neat guide.

6 Spoon out the meringue mix on to the circle.

7 Cook the meringue for one hour or until it is set. Turn off the oven and allow to cool completely.

8 Transfer to a serving platter.

Topping

1 Whip the cream or combine the mascarpone and yoghurt with a fork, and spread it over the meringue.

2 Scatter over the chopped pistachio nuts and dried petals.

3 Add the fresh rose petals and drizzle with the rose syrup just before serving.

Serves 8

Meringue base
4 egg whites
200g (1 cup) caster sugar
2 tsp rose water (see page 88 in Culinary Extras)

Topping
500ml (17fl oz) double or heavy cream or equivalent amount of mascarpone and plain yoghurt
1 handful chopped pistachio nuts
1 handful fresh rose petals
1 handful dried rose petals
100ml (3fl oz) rose syrup (see page 79 in Culinary Extras)

Helianthus annuus
Sunflower

A hardy annual with edible flower buds, petals and seeds

HEIGHT & SPREAD 100 x 40cm (39 x 16in)

Sunflowers magically conjure up the feeling of summer. They remind us of holidays and heat but for many people they are also reminiscent of childhood. This is because they are the ideal starter flower — if you want to encourage anyone, of any age, to take an interest in gardening then give them a packet of sunflower seeds.

Sow the seed in pots or directly into the ground in late spring or under cover in the autumn and germination is guaranteed. They like to be in a sunny open position with plenty of space around them. Too close to their neighbours and they are more likely to attract snails and slugs. Varieties with very large heads may need staking, but generally they are able to support themselves just as they do in fields where they are grown as productive crops. Replicating similar conditions will result in tough robust plants that need little cosseting. They only require minimal water if the soil around them starts to dry out.

If the primary bright yellow faces of the standard varieties are too much of a statement for a grown-up planting scheme, then look at some of the more sedate types that are the results of recent breeding programmes — those with cream, bronze or claret-coloured petals are chic and elegant with smaller flower heads. My preference is for 'Ms Mars' as it fits in better with the other plants in my garden but it is rewarding and inexpensive to experiment with a few different seed packets for a rainbow mix of petal colours that will look stunning on a plate.

Pick your petals first thing in the morning when they are fresh. Gently remove them individually from the head, leaving this intact on the plant as it is full of seeds that need more growing time to mature and ripen. The seeds are ready to harvest when they are plump and loose. Shake them into a paper bag and allow them to dry out completely — the inner kernel is the edible part. You will need to crack open the outer casing to retrieve this. Both the seeds and petals have a nutty flavour. The seeds are particularly high in vitamin E and selenium. Use in stews, soups, breads, dips, butters and home-made granola or eat them raw as a snack. Add the petals to any vegetable dish. You can also eat the young buds of sunflowers. Known as chokes on restaurant menus, they are reminiscent in texture to artichoke hearts. Pick them before the petals appear and use in the same way — either steamed or roasted.

SUNFLOWER BEAN DIP WITH RUSTIC SUNFLOWER BREADSTICKS

Makes 12 breadsticks

Breadsticks

1 Combine the dry ingredients including half the sunflower seeds in a bowl and make a well.

2 Add the water and sunflower oil and mix with a spoon until you have a soft, slightly sticky dough. Add more water or flour if it seems too wet or dry.

3 Lightly flour a worktop or wooden board and knead the dough for 10 minutes.

4 Place the dough in a clean bowl and cover with a tea towel for 30 minutes until it rises slightly.

5 Divide the dough into twelve balls and roll each ball between your palms until you have a thick sausage-shaped breadstick. Place the breadsticks on a greased baking tray and cover with the tea towel for a further 15 minutes.

6 Preheat the oven to 200°C/400°F/Gas Mark 6.

7 Remove the tea towel and sprinkle the remaining sunflower seeds over the top of the breadsticks.

8 Bake for 15–20 minutes (check after 10) until cooked.

9 They will keep in an airtight tin for three days.

Dip

1 Warm half the sunflower oil in a pan and add the chopped garlic.

2 Cook until soft and add the cannellini beans.

3 Squeeze over the lemon juice and keep on the heat until the beans are soft.

4 Place all the ingredients in a blender with the remaining sunflower oil and whizz until everything is smooth and creamy.

5 Transfer to a small bowl, allow to cool and stir in the sunflower seeds.

Breadsticks
2 tbsp sunflower seeds
250g (2¼ cups) wholemeal flour
½ sachet instant yeast
1 tsp sea salt
160ml (6fl oz) warm water
1½ tbsp sunflower oil

Dip
I 400g tin (4 cups) of drained cannellini beans
2 tbsp sunflower oil
2 cloves of garlic, finely chopped
Juice of 1 lemon
1 tbsp sunflower seeds
Handful of fresh sunflower petals for serving

Tropaeolum majus
Nasturtium

A hardy annual with edible flowers, leaves and seeds

HEIGHT & SPREAD 30 x 45cm (12 x 18in)

My number one plant for starting an edible flower garden is the nasturtium. It is especially useful as all its parts are edible. Once considered a stalwart of traditional cottage gardens, the brightly coloured flowers and delicately veined, lily-pad-shaped leaves look stunning in the border and on the plate. The subdued colours of 'Black Velvet' work well in a modern outdoor setting or mix them up with the primary colours of 'Tom Thumb' and plant a container brimming with nasturtiums outside the kitchen door.

They are the easiest plants in the world to grow from seed — the knobbly nubs can be handled individually between your finger and thumb and are easily poked into the soil to a depth of 5cm (2in). If you space them evenly apart at about 15cm (6in), there will be no need for any thinning out. They are not fussy so you can use any kind of soil or compost. Sow in late spring as soon as the ground has warmed up and germination will be very quick.

Both the flowers and leaves are edible and delicious — the flowers have a delicate peppery flavour and add texture, colour and crunch to a mixed green salad. The leaves can be coated in a light batter and deep fried in vegetable oil to serve as a tempura or whizzed in the blender to make a vivid pesto for dressing pasta.

Several plants and staggered sowing times mean you will have flowers and foliage to pick all summer long. As the flowers fade you will notice large fat seed pods appearing in their place. These are also edible and are commonly known as 'poor man's capers'. They have the distinctive tangy flavour and taste of traditional capers and should be harvested whilst still soft, covered with cool, boiled white wine vinegar and decanted into a sterilized, sealed jar. They will be ready to eat after a month.

At the end of the flowering season leave some of the pods to ripen on the plant. Although nasturtiums have a self-seeding tendency it's worth saving some seed for sowing again. Wait until they have turned brown and hard — do not attempt to pickle them at this stage but save in a cool dark place until the following spring ready for planting.

NASTURTIUM TRIO

Nasturtium leaf tempura

1 Beat all the ingredients, minus the egg white, together with a fork until you have a thick paste.

2 Allow to rest for half an hour.

3 Add the beaten egg white.

4 Dip the nasturtium leaves into the batter ensuring they are fully coated on both sides.

5 Cook them in a deep pan of hot oil for a few minutes, holding them under with a spatula until they are golden and crisp.

6 Set out on a piece of kitchen paper to drain.

Stuffed flowers

1 To fill the flowers, remove the stamens (see page 18) and insert the cream cheese using a very small teaspoon or the smallest nozzle of an icing bag.

2 Assemble on a plate with the pickled seedpods and the stuffed flowers.

Serves 6 as an appetizer

Nasturtium leaf tempura
100g (1 cup) plain flour
2 tbsp light vegetable cooking oil
175ml (7fl oz) sparkling mineral water
1 stiffly beaten egg white
10–12 freshly picked nasturtium leaves (If you pick them earlier in the day, keep them in a sealed container in the fridge to make sure they stay completely firm and dry.)

Stuffed flowers
10 nasturtium flowers,
Small portion of oregano flower cream cheese (see page 104 in Culinary Extras)
1 portion of pickled nasturtium seed pods (see page 73)

Culinary extras

This chapter contains a list of suggestions for using your home-grown edible flowers in cooking and food preparation. However, these are only suggestions and once you become familiar with the flowers that are safe to eat there are myriad ways to incorporate them into your own everyday recipes. The more accustomed you become to using edible flowers as an ingredient, the more you will want to experiment with their different flavours, tastes and textures.

Syrup of roses: scented, sweet and delicious

Floral syrups

To make a floral syrup add a few handfuls of your chosen flowers to a saucepan of sugar syrup. Using strongly scented flowers will provide the best results. As a guide these are the quantities you will need:

Elderflower syrup: 10 heads of elderflower for each cup of water

Violet syrup: 3 cups of sweet violet flowers for each cup of water

Lilac syrup: 2 cups of lilac florets for each cup of water

Rose syrup: 2 cups of rose petals for each cup of water

Lavender syrup: 45ml (3 tbsp) of lavender flowers for each cup of water

Flower syrups form the basis of many floral recipes. They are a way of bottling the fragrance of a flower – not unlike making perfume – and provide a means of converting the original scent into a taste. Rather than distilling the natural essential oils, which is done through steam extraction in the production of perfume, it is possible to capture the scent by steeping flowers in warm water and preserve it by adding sugar. If possible, pick flowers at their headiest when they have had the warmth of the sun on them. Once bottled, flower syrups will keep for a year.

1   Make your syrup using equal parts sugar and water (one cup of water and one cup of sugar), and bring to a simmer in a saucepan until the sugar has dissolved and the syrup starts to thicken.

2   Remove from the heat and add your flowers, making sure they are all covered in the syrup. Allow to cool overnight.

3   Decant into sterilized bottles or jars (see page 80) and seal.

4   Strain if you want a clear-coloured syrup or leave in some petals for a pretty effect. Label and store in a cool dark place.

5   Once open keep refrigerated. Use within a week.

Fruits

Flowers and fruits have an easy affinity and they naturally complement each other, which is not surprising as all fruits start their life as flowers. Scatter freshly picked petals over a summer fruit salad of red berries and sprinkle with your favourite floral sugar and the juice of half a lemon. Use diluted flower cordials and syrups to bake or poach fruits in lieu of water. Rhubarb (technically a vegetable but cooks like a fruit) and roses make the perfect marriage or try apples and lilac or plums and beebalm – fruits are perfect for experimenting with a new range of flavour combinations, mixing what's in season with preserved and dried flower flavours. See page 50 for hibiscus poached pears.

Honeys

Unflavoured, clear shop-bought runny honeys can be used to make flower-favoured honeys with home-grown blooms. Use scented flowers such as honeysuckles, jasmine, lilac, sweet violets, roses or dianthus, as seen opposite.

1   To make a floral honey pour a jar of unflavoured runny honey into a small jug.

2   Place a layer of freshly picked scented flower petals in the bottom of the original jar and pour a small amount of honey back in.

3   Add another layer of petals and repeat with the poured honey until you have filled the jar back up.

4   Finish with a layer of petals on top and seal with the original jar lid. The petals will gradually impart their scent and flavour to the honey. It will keep for six months.

STERILIZING JARS

Glass jars and bottles can be sterilized in a dishwasher. Remove rubber seals and lids, place on the top rack and run on a hot wash. Do not use any detergent. Time the cycle to finish when you are ready to fill your jars.

You can also place empty jars with no lids or seals in a microwave. Wash in clean soapy water, put wet jars in the microwave and cook on high for 60 seconds. Or put clean wet jars in a preheated over at 180°C/350°F/Gas Mark 4 for about 15 minutes.

A jar of runny honey made with layers of dianthus petals

Jams

Making your own floral jam is a lovely way of capturing and preserving the best floral scents from your garden. Pick flowers when they are in full bloom and their perfume is at their headiest.

To make a few pots of floral jam you will need:

5 handfuls of freshly picked, scented flower heads or petals of your choice – best results are obtained from jasmine, roses, dianthus, lavender, violets and lilac
460g (2 cups) preserving sugar or granulated sugar
Juice from 2 lemons
750ml (25½fl oz) cold water
Sterilized jam jars (see page 80)

1   Wash your flowers or petals by dipping them in a bowl of cold water and carefully pat dry with a soft tea cloth or absorbent kitchen paper.

2   Put the flowers in a bowl and sprinkle with half the sugar and lemon juice.

3   Cover and leave to rest for a minimum of 2 hours but ideally overnight.

4   Bring the water to a boil over medium heat.

5   Add the remaining sugar and lemon and simmer gently until the sugar has dissolved.

6   Add your flowers in small amounts and stir very gently. Simmer gently for 20 minutes.

7   Bring to the boil again until a setting point is reached. Your mixture will start to thicken.

8   Do not be alarmed if your flowers turn brown. It is the flavour that counts for jam, and this will be released into the hot mixture.

9   Leave to settle for a few minutes and then spoon into your jar. Seal immediately and store in a cold place. It will keep for several months.

THE SETTING POINT FOR JAM
The setting point for jam is 105°C/220°F. You can test this with a sugar thermometer or you can use the wrinkle test: spoon a little jam on to a cold heatproof plate. Leave for a minute and then push with your finger. If it wrinkles then it has set. If it is still liquid, boil the jam for another 5 minutes before testing again.

Jellies

Make jellies with floral cordials and waters (see pages 84 and 88) to create your own flowery flavours and pretty them up by adding freshly picked petals and small blooms with whatever happens to be in season.

Makes 4

200ml (7fl oz) flower cordial (see page 84 for recipe)
4 sheets of leaf gelatine or 2 sachets gelatine powder
200ml (7fl oz) sparkling white wine, champagne or non-alcoholic equivalent
4 individual glass dishes for serving
Fresh flowers for decoration

SPARKLING FLORAL JELLIES

1   Soak the gelatine leaves in cold water until soft. Squeeze the leaves and discard the water or dissolve the gelatine powder in a cup with 45ml (3 tbsp) warm water. Follow the packet instructions and quantities in both cases for accuracy.

2   Pour the floral cordial and half the sparkling wine into a pan and heat until it is just simmering.

3   Add the gelatine and stir until it has dissolved.

4   Pour into a large jug and gently stir in the remaining sparkling wine retaining the bubbles.

5   Put some freshly picked edible flowers or petals in the bottom of each glass dish.

6   Pour the jelly mixture over the flowers dividing equally between each dish.

7   Cover and refrigerate until set.

8   The flowers will float to the top but will set in the jelly.

9   Add more flowers to the tops of the jellies if desired before serving.

Floral cordials

To make a floral cordial of your choice use a handful of freshly picked scented petals or flowers. Honeysuckle, lilac, hibiscus, elderflower, rose or jasmine all make delicious, refreshing cordials.

Handful of freshly picked
  scented petals or flowers
900g (4½ cups) granulated
  sugar
1 lemon, sliced
2 litres (3½ pints) still
  mineral water

1   Put the petals in a large bowl with the granulated sugar, a sliced lemon and the still mineral water.

2   Cover with a clean cloth and leave to infuse for 24 hours, stirring occasionally.

3   Strain the liquid through a sieve and decant into sterilized glass bottles (see page 80). Seal and refrigerate. Use within 2 weeks.

If you want to serve as a long drink, dilute with sparkling or still water. Keep some bottles aside for using in jellies, cocktails and sweet batters.

Crystallized/ frosted flowers

This is the prettiest way to decorate cakes, cookies and desserts for a special occasion. Choose scented flowers for the best results: lavender heads, small roses and rose petals, violets and dianthus.

1 egg white
Approximately 400g (2 cups)
  caster sugar
2 handfuls of edible flower
  petals and/or small edible
  flower heads

1   Whisk the egg white until light and fluffy.

2   Use a small paintbrush to coat the flowers and petals back and front with the egg white.

3   Sprinkle the sugar evenly over the flowers and place them on a tray lined with greaseproof paper.

4   Leave to dry overnight on a plate. No need to refrigerate. Once they are hard, store in an airtight container. The sugar coating will preserve the flowers for several months.

A jug of garnet-coloured hibiscus cordial

Petal confetti for decoration

It is easy to make your own dried petal confetti to use as instant decoration. The colourful mix of tiny petals from flowers such as marigolds, zinnias, African daisies and sunflowers, add a vibrant finish to cakes, cookies and desserts.

To make, remove the petals from the individual flower heads and lay out on a plate or tray to dry naturally in a warm place away from direct sunlight (see page 116). They will usually dry in 24 hours. Store in an airtight jar for scattering over plain icing, cream cheese frosting or royal icing before it sets. Edible confetti will last for up to a year.

Makes 20

90g (¾ stick) softened butter
100g (½ cup) floral sugar (see page 92)
1 egg
200g (2 cups) plain flour
½ tsp baking powder
½ tsp floral salt (see page 96)

PETAL CONFETTI COOKIES

1   Preheat the oven to 180°C/350°F/Gas Mark 4.

2   Cream the butter and sugar together.

3   Beat in the egg.

4   In a separate bowl, combine the flour, baking powder and salt.

5   Add the dry ingredients to the creamed butter and egg.

6   Mix to form a dough; cover and leave it to rest in the fridge for an hour.

7   Roll out the dough on a floured work surface to a thickness of ½cm (¼in).

8   Cut out cookies with a flower-shaped cutter and place on a greased baking sheet.

9   Bake for 10 minutes or so until the cookies are golden.

10 Remove from the oven and allow to cool.

11 Ice and scatter with edible petal confetti.

Chocolate

Dark chocolate and edible scented flowers are perfect together. Use scented floral syrups in chocolate cakes, mousses, brownies and muffins or replace ordinary caster sugar with a floral sugar. Fresh rose petals dipped in dark chocolate are an especially delicious treat.

Makes up to 20

Two or three large scented rose flowers in full bloom
100g (3½ oz) bar of dark chocolate
50ml (1½fl oz) rose syrup (see page 79)
Coarse sea salt or pink Himalayan salt

1 Gently remove the petals from the main flower head.

2 Reserve the largest and remove the white heel at the base of the petal with a pair of small scissors. If you try to remove it by hand you are likely to tear the whole petal and this needs to stay intact.

3 Place your petals in a sealed bag or container and refrigerate for a couple of hours or until they are slightly stiff.

4 In a bain-marie melt the chocolate – break it into small squares to speed up the process.

5 When the chocolate has melted, remove from the heat and stir in the rose syrup.

6 Dip the bottom half of each rose petal into the melted chocolate.

7 Place on a tray or plate lined with greaseproof paper and sprinkle with a few grains of salt before the chocolate sets.

Substitute rose petals for sprigs of lavender or small florets of lilac, and provide a dipping bowl of melted chocolate for a flower fondue.

Flavoured waters and unsweetened juices

Although rose water will be the first floral water to spring to mind, you can make any kind of floral or herbal water with scented edible flowers or herbs. Flavoured waters can be used in sweet or savoury batters, dressings and marinades or mixed with icing sugar to drizzle over fruit salads or as frosting for cakes.

Follow these instructions and substitute the rose petals for others of your choice.

1   Add a handful of clean rose petals to a saucepan.

2   Just cover the petals with mineral water.

3   Place the pan on the stove on low heat and cover the pan with a lid.

4   Simmer for 30–45 minutes until the petals lose their colour. Do not allow to boil.

5   Leave the rose water to cool completely.

6   Strain and pour into sterilized glass bottles (see page 80). Keep in the fridge.

Teas and tisanes

You can make floral and herbal teas and tisanes from any edible flowers, herbs and foliage, and from some of the edible seeds listed in the directory on page 120. Pouring hot, boiled water over flowers, leaves or seeds releases their taste and aroma and is the best way to capture any nutritional benefits. You can judge quantities according to taste, but generally a small handful of petals or seeds or one or two leaves is enough for one person. If making a pot, increase the amounts. Strain any liquid before drinking.

You can also flavour black or green tea leaves by layering them in a sealed container with perfumed flowers or foliage of your choice. Allow a few days for the tea leaves to take on the flavour.

Jasmine-flavoured water for both sweet and savoury dishes

Creams and custards

Add flavoured floral syrup, cordial, water and sugar to whipping cream and custard for cake and meringue fillings or use as an ingredient for cream-based desserts such as mousses, panna cottas and crème brûlées. You can add more flowers for decoration.

Makes 6

570ml (1 pint) double or heavy cream
½ tbsp floral syrup (see page 79)
6 egg yolks
50g (⅓ cup) caster sugar
4 tsp cornflour

For the floral caramel
200g (1⅓ cup) floral sugar (see page 92)

FLORAL CRÈME BRÛLÉE

1   Beat the egg yolks, cornflour, floral syrup and sugar in a bowl.

2   Add the cream to a pan and bring to boiling point.

3   Remove from the heat and pour over the sugared egg yolks, beating all the time.

4   Return the mixture to the pan and cook over a low heat for ten minutes or so until it thickens to a custard-like consistency.

5   Divide between six small ramekins or teacups and leave to cool.

6   Refrigerate overnight.

7   Make the caramel topping once you have removed the ramekins from the fridge. To make the caramel, place the floral sugar in a pan over a very low heat until it dissolves and caramelizes. This takes about ten minutes. Pour the caramel over the custards and leave for a few minutes to harden.

Cakes and muffins

Replacing standard ingredients with floral syrup, sugar and butter in cake and muffin recipes rings the changes and breaks up any monotony that comes from using the same ingredients repeatedly. To make a floral cake see the recipe for pellie cake on page 62.

Makes 8

40g (¾ stick) melted unsalted butter
100g (1 cup) plain flour
¼ tsp bicarbonate of soda
1 tsp baking powder
40g (⅓ cup) caster sugar
Pinch of salt
50ml (1½ fl oz) plain yoghurt
50ml (1½ fl oz) milk
1 egg
10g (¼ cup mixed home-grown edible flower seeds
8 muffin cases on a baking tray

SEEDED MUFFINS

1   Preheat the oven to 200°C/400°F/Gas Mark 6.

2   Combine the flour, bicarbonate of soda, baking powder, sugar, salt and seeds in a bowl.

3   Beat the melted butter, yoghurt, milk and egg in a jug and pour on to the dry ingredients.

4   Mix gently.

5   Spoon into the muffin cases and bake for around 20 minutes. They are cooked when they are golden and firm on top.

Meringues

For individual floral meringues adapt the rose pavlova recipe on page 66. Use any flavour of floral sugar (see page 92) in lieu of plain sugar, and colour with natural food colouring. Swirl a small amount through the egg and sugar mixture. With a dessert or a tablespoon, place mini heaped hillocks on a lined and greased baking tray, well spaced out. Scatter with petals and cook on a low heat, 130°C/220°F/Gas Mark 2, until firm. Turn the oven off and leave to cool completely before removing.

Macaroons

Make your own flower-flavoured macaroons by adding 1 tsp floral water of your choice (see page 88).

Makes 20

150g (2¼ cups) ground
  almonds
200g (1 cup) caster sugar
2 egg whites
1 tsp floral water
1 tsp food colouring (optional)
1 tbsp plain flour
20 crystallized flowers for
  decoration (see page 84)

1   Cream the ground almonds, caster sugar and egg whites.

2   Add the flour, food colouring and floral water and mix together so the mixture turns into a paste. Place in the fridge for an hour.

3   Flour a work surface and your hands, and roll small amounts of the mixture into small balls between the palms of your hands.

4   Flatten into rounds and place on a lined baking tray. Bake for 10–15 minutes in a warm oven 160°C/320°F/Gas Mark 3.

5   Allow to cool and add a crystallized flower for decoration before hardening. Leave for 15 minutes before eating.

Floral sugars

To prepare any floral sugar, chop perfumed flowers (such as beebalm, lilac or lavender), herbs (such as rosemary, mint, hyssop, lemon balm or sweet cicely) or scented foliage (such as pelargonium or myrtle leaves) as finely as possible, removing any hard stalks from the leaves. You will need 1 tablespoon of chopped ingredients to 225g (1¼ cups) of caster sugar. You can combine these in a pestle and mortar, crushing the petals or leaves to release their scent, or you can do this in a liquidizer or spice grinder, which will result in a soft powdery sugar but is the best way to colour the sugar uniformly if this is the result you are after.

Decant into a clear jam jar and shake well. The sugar will gradually take on the flavour of your flowers, becoming stronger over time as the natural oils disperse. Floral sugar will keep for about six months although the colour will gradually fade.

Pelargonium sugar takes on the colour and scent of the foliage.

Granola

Add edible flowers and seeds of your choice to create your own home-made bespoke granola. Serve with plain yoghurt or kefir and poached fruit for breakfast or as a dessert.

Makes 5 generous servings

200g (3 cups) rolled oats
150ml (5fl oz) olive or other
   vegetable oil
1 tbsp clear or floral infused
   honey (see page 80)
1 large handful of sunflower
   seeds
I small handful linseeds
1 small handful poppy seeds
1 small handful nigella seeds
1 small handful caraway seeds
I handful of flaked almonds or
   other chopped nuts
I tsp cinnamon powder
1 handful dried edible petals
   (see page 116)
Coarse sea salt

1   Preheat the oven to 130°C/220°F/Gas Mark 2.

2   Place the rolled oats in a large bowl.

3   Combine the honey and oil in a jar, mixing with a spoon until you have a syrupy liquid.

4   Pour over the oats and stir well until every grain is coated.

5   Add the seeds, one portion at a time, stirring well to combine.

6   Add the nuts.

7   Stir in the cinnamon powder.

8   Spread the mixture thinly on a foil-lined baking tray.

9   Sprinkle with sea salt.

10 Transfer to the oven and bake for about an hour until the oats are golden and toasted.

11 Leave to cool, mix in the dried edible petals and transfer to a sealed container. It will keep for several weeks.

Ice creams and gelati

If you have an ice cream maker, the world is your oyster when it comes to experimenting with a wide variety of floral or herbal ice creams. Follow a standard recipe and trial new flavour combinations with whatever is in season in your garden.

For an easy, refreshing no-churn ice cream use crème fraiche and a floral or herbal sugar. Combine 100g (1 cup) of floral sugar (see page 92) and a large tub of crème fraiche in a bowl. Fold in three beaten egg whites and transfer to a freezer container. Freeze for at least four hours before serving. Will keep for several weeks in the freezer.

Granitas and sorbets

Floral and herbal granitas make wonderful palate cleansers served as small portions between courses of a heavy meal or in larger portions as light and refreshing desserts. They are quick and easy to make if you have a prepared bottle of syrup.

Serves 6

250ml (7fl oz) floral syrup
(see page 79)
100ml (3fl oz) water
Juice of 1 lemon

GRANITA

1   Dilute the floral syrup with the water and pour into a shallow freezer-proof container.

2   Add the lemon juice.

3   Seal the container and place in the freezer.

4   Leave overnight and the following morning use a fork to break up the flavoured ice into small crunchy crystals.

5   Refreeze until you are ready to serve. Use within a couple of days.

SORBET

Turn your granita into a sorbet by folding two stiffly beaten egg whites into the ice crystals.

Floral and herbal salts

Make floral or herbal salts to use on dishes and in recipes in place of ordinary salt – the brightly coloured petals of cornflowers, French marigolds or clover will add some real zing to a plate of fried potatoes or scrambled egg. If you want to flavour the salt then use herb flowers. Thyme, oregano, sage, coriander and tarragon will imbue the salt with their flavour. Salt will preserve the flower colours and you can pick them out of the salt if you want to use more flowers than salt in dressings or marinades. Just add a new batch of flowers to the original salt. It is better to use dried flower petals rather than fresh to keep the salt moisture free.

Pack the petals or herbs in an airtight jar between layers of sea or rock salt. It will last up to six months.

Breadsticks

See recipe for breadsticks on page 70. You can substitute the sunflower seeds with any other edible seeds: nigella, linseed or poppy seeds.

Breads

If you make your own bread it is easy to combine flowers into the doughs of soft breads such as focaccia and fougasse. Follow a basic recipe and use flower heads and leaves to press into the dough before it goes into the oven.

You can also show off your garden-grown flowers by making a flower garlic loaf: use a floral or herbal butter (see page 98) and two cloves of diced garlic. Combine the butter and garlic and cut diagonal incisions into a baguette or a similar long shaped bread. Spoon the butter into the cuts and smear any remaining butter over the top. Wrap in foil and bake in the oven at 200°C/400°F/Gas Mark 6 for ten minutes or so. Scatter more edible flowers over the top once it is out of the oven.

To make pretty fresh flower sandwiches use a floral butter to spread on both sides of two even slices of white or wholemeal bread. Add more flowers to one side and then make your sandwich. Cut in half or in triangles so you can see the flower filling.

SEEDED FLATBREADS

Makes 4

200g (1¾ cup) plain flour
¼ tsp salt
2 tbsp sunflower oil
250g (1 cup) natural yoghurt
Generous handful mixed edible
    seeds

1   Place the flour, salt and seeds in a large bowl.

2   Add the oil and yoghurt. Stir everything together to make a dough and knead for a few minutes. You are aiming for a soft dough. If it is too sticky, add a little more flour or if it is too dry, add a splash of water.

3   Leave the dough to stand for about 30 minutes.

4   Divide the dough into four and shape into balls.

5   On a clean floured surface roll each ball into a round circular shape, about 1cm (½ inch) thick.

6   Heat a large frying pan.

7   Take a sheet of kitchen paper and rub a little oil on to the surface of the pan.

8   Add your flatbreads one at a time to the hot pan and cook on each side for about 2 minutes. Eat immediately.

Edible seeds are packed full of nutrients which function as antioxidants: they taste delicious and actually do you good!

Pickles

To ring the changes with a basic pickle recipe, consider adding a couple of dessert spoons of elderflower cordial in lieu of sugar.

Combine 300ml (11fl oz) white wine vinegar, 20ml (2 dessert spoons) of elderflower cordial, a pinch of caraway seeds and ¼ tsp of rock salt. Mix well and add a small handful of edible herb or vegetable flowers – borage, broad bean, rocket, celery and parsley flowers all work well here. Chill for at least 40 minutes to pickle.

The pickle will keep in the fridge for a couple of days. You can use it to dress fish and chicken dishes or whisk 2 tablespoons of olive oil into the pickle liquid to make a salad dressing.

See page 46 for pickled fennel flower recipe.

Butters

Butter boards are having a moment. Follow the trend by making sweetly flavoured flower butters for spreading directly on to toast or bread or to use in cake, cookie and other batter recipes. Use herb flowers, edible foliage or seeds to make savoury butters.

Use fresh or dried flowers or foliage – about one small handful of flowers to 110g (1 stick) softened butter. Use whole flowers with small heads such as daisies, violas or borage or remove individual petals from large flowers such as chrysanthemums, Sulphur cosmos or mallows.

In a shallow bowl use a knife to layer up the butter with the flowers or stir in seeds with a spoon. Use a glass bowl for maximum visual effect. Press down gently and cover.

Refrigerate until it becomes a solid pat.

Pickled fennel flowers with fennel seeds, fronds and stalks

Soups and broths

Home-made vegetable soups can be flavoured with vegetable and herb flowers. If you are making a pea soup it makes sense to include some beautiful home-grown pea flowers. The same goes for courgettes (zucchini). You will get more flavour if you use them from the start of the cooking process but then they will lose some of their colour. Ideally use half at the beginning and reserve half to add at the end.

You can also use flower or herb-based stocks (see recipe opposite) as the base for your soups.

Adding freshly picked summer flowers to chilled soup and gazpacho means there is no chance of them losing their colour and they will not wilt if the soup is served cold. To make, blitz a diced cucumber, a handful of borage flowers, the juice of one lemon, two cups of plain yoghurt, a cup of water and some chive leaves until smooth. Season with salt and pepper. Chill and serve very cold. Float more borage and chive flowers on top for decoration. Eat immediately.

CHRYSANTHEMUM BROTH

Serves 4

1 litre (2 pints) hot vegetable stock
1 generous tsp white miso paste
4 spring onions, finely sliced
1 tsp diced ginger
1 red chilli, finely sliced with seeds removed
4 sprigs coriander
4 chrysanthemum flower heads
1 generous handful chrysanthemum petals
soya sauce to taste

1   Bring the vegetable stock to the boil and add the miso paste.

2   Stir well until it is incorporated, and add the ginger, spring onions and chilli.

3   Cook for a few minutes.

4   In the meantime, divide the chrysanthemum petals between four bowls.

5   Ladle the broth into the bowls and add a flower head to each one.

6   Garnish with the coriander sprigs and add soya sauce to taste.

Stock

It is easy to enhance the flavour of a basic stock recipe by adding savoury aromatic flowers.

Take a celery stalk, celery leaves and celery flowers, half an onion, a carrot, a handful of peppercorns and a pinch of salt plus a handful of flowers of your choice such as onion flowers, chive flowers, coriander or rocket flowers and place in a saucepan. Cover with 500ml (17fl oz) of cold water and bring to the boil for ten minutes. Strain through a sieve and taste. If you think the flavour needs to be more concentrated, put it back on the boil and simmer without a lid so the liquid evaporates and the stock reduces in volume. You can then adjust the seasoning by adding more salt. Your stock will form the basis for soups and stews, casseroles and risottos.

To make a single note stock use dried flowers and foliage such as calendula. Place a handful of dried petals and a few leaves in a spice grinder or use a pestle and mortar and break them down until they form a powder. You will need several teaspoons to dilute with boiling water to make a litre (2 pints) of stock. Season with salt and pepper to taste. The powder will last for several months.

Dips

Flowers can easily be incorporated into home-made or shop-bought dips and spreads. For easy dips, combine Greek yoghurt and cream cheese in equal quantities. You can add diced cucumber and garlic for a riff on tzatziki and stir in a handful of borage flowers and calendula petals. Alternatively, use cottage cheese and plain yoghurt and mix in some mint flowers, garlic flowers or chive flowers. Season and chill dips before serving with a plate of raw vegetable crudites. Eat within 24 hours.

For sunflower bean dip see recipe on page 70.

Stir-fries and risottos

Using flowers, foliage and seeds in stir fries and risotto or other rice-based dishes will liven up everyday meals and bring new and unexpected flavours to your cooking. The blandness of rice and noodles means that the tastes of any new or unusual ingredient can be easily discerned on the palate. Use whatever you have to hand in the garden but avoid overly sweet scented flowers. Hyssop will provide a gentle aniseed flavour, lemon verbena a citrus note, jasmine has a musky taste and calendula a zesty grassiness.

See page 38 for calendula risotto recipe.

Pasta

If you make your own pasta you can use fresh or dried flowers in the dough. Quick cooking times mean that they will hold up as long as they are fully incorporated. If you don't have a pasta machine, it is possible to cheat: layer some flower petals between two sheets of shop-bought lasagne and brush down with a smear of oil. Roll the pasta and remove the top sheet. The flowers will be stuck to the bottom sheet and should remain there for cooking. Use immediately.

Salads

Mixed flower garden salads or green leaf salads topped with edible flowers are the best entry point for eating freshly picked flowers. Avoid using sweetly scented blooms and stick to aromatic herb flowers and mix with vibrant edible flowers such as snapdragons, fuschias, bizzie lizzies and begonias that tend to be blander in taste and reminiscent of lettuce. It is the textures and freshness that count in a salad. For a kick of flavour use allium or chive florets, or garlic or mustard flowers, and add foliage such as nasturtium or dandelion leaves for some peppery undertones.

Calendula risotto made with calendula stock and calendula flowers.

Pizza and savoury pastry dough bases	As with the cheat's pasta, roll fresh or dried nasturtium or herb flowers into your dough and brush with a little oil. Use light toppings of onions or leeks so you can see the flowers in the dough base once cooked and add more flowers for decoration once cooking is complete.
Flower and herb cheeses	Cheeses such as ricotta, soft goat's cheese or any other creamy spreadable cheese can be easily decorated with flowers: sprinkle a thin layer of edible flowers on to a small sheet of greaseproof paper. Spoon the soft cheese on top and smooth out with a knife into a small rectangular shape. Using the bottom corners of the paper, start to roll gently so the cheese forms a sausage shape and the outside edges are covered in petals. Twist the bottom and top ends of the paper together and place in the fridge for a couple of hours. Remove the paper before serving.
Omelettes, frittatas and scrambled eggs	You can combine edible flowers and herbs to all manner of egg-based dishes. Add a handful of petals right at the end of the cooking so they do not turn brown. They look especially stunning in a rolled omelette once it is sliced. Alternatively, use fresh petals or small flower heads as a garnish. Dahlia, fuchsia, begonia and nasturtium flowers all complement the taste of eggs.

Oils

To make a herbal oil, use 500ml (17fl oz) of light vegetable oil as a carrier. Avoid using nut oils or even olive oil as they already have their own distinctive flavour. Stand several stems of flowering herbs in a sterilizied bottle or jar (see page 80) and simply pour the oil over the top. Allow a week for the flavour to infuse. It will last up to six months.

Vinegars

To make a floral vinegar you will need 500ml (17fl oz) white wine vinegar, a handful of freshly picked scented edible flowers for a sweet vinegar or herb flowers for a sharp vinegar, and a sterilized jar or bottle (see page 80) with a lid for sealing.

Gently warm the vinegar over a low heat, add the flowers to the jar or bottle.

Pour the vinegar over the flowers and seal immediately. Leave for a week to infuse and then strain into another sterilized bottle. Use in dressings and marinades. It will keep up to six months.

Dressings

Combine two parts flavoured oil with one part flavoured vinegar, a squeeze of lemon juice and salt and pepper to taste. It is useful to keep a dressing in the fridge for regular use. It will keep for up to a week.

Wait until your guests have admired the salad and taken a picture before dressing a flower salad; otherwise the flowers will wilt. Ideally serve the dressing from a small jug and allow everyone to dress their own salad.

Viola ice cubes in sparkling elderflower cordial.

Ice cubes and lollies

This is an easy way to preserve edible flowers if you want to use them at a later stage. Simply turn them into ice cubes and add to soups, stocks and broths as required. Alternatively, once frozen, use immediately in cold drinks for visual impact.

Simply place small flower heads or petals in an ice tray and half fill with cold water. Freeze and when ice begins to form fill the tray up to the top. This keeps the flowers fixed in the centre of the cube.

Use the same method for making lollies with edible flowers in them. Fill a lolly mould a quarter of the way with diluted syrup or cordial and add flowers. Freeze and repeat.

Cocktails and champagnes

To make a floral cocktail, stir or shake 1 part flower syrup of your choice (see page 79), 1 part dry vermouth and 6 parts vodka in a mixing glass or cocktail shaker with ice cubes. Pour into a chilled cocktail glass and garnish with an edible flower.

To make a floral champagne, add 1 part flower syrup to the bottom of a champagne flute and top up with champagne or sparkling white wine. Stir well so the colour mixes in. Garnish with an edible flower.

Garnishes

Use any beautiful garden-grown edible flowers that don't have a strong enough flavour to earn their place as a single note ingredient as garnishes. Think of your serving platters as alternative vases for arranging food and flowers together to create eye-catching displays that will instantly make everything look a hundred times more appetizing.

The floral pantry

Stocking your larder, fridge and freezer with supplies of edible flowers means you are more likely to use them on a regular basis in your cooking. Different types of plants hold up to freezing and drying and you will mostly discover which ones work best through trial and error. Bear in mind that drying and pressing will change the colour and texture of your flowers and individual petals or tiny flowers withstand freezing better than the heads of large fleshy blooms. Freshly picked flowers will last in the fridge for up to a week.

How to store, dry and preserve edible flowers

In my dreams I live in an old rambling house — the kind of place with a series of rooms off a large airy kitchen. One of these is a scullery for conditioning my freshly picked flowers, and another is a pantry lined with sturdy wooden shelves housing rows of glass jars filled with jams, syrups and other floral preserves and condiments — all the results of the past season's harvest. Beautiful bunches of dried flowers are suspended from the ceiling waiting to be used at a moment's notice in my food prep. The truth, of course, is that like most people my home has limited storage space, but that doesn't stop me from finding ways to make my edible garden-grown flowers last so I can use them year-round.

Fridge

Freshly picked flowers can be stored in the fridge for up to a week. Pick your flowers when they are completely moisture free — midday or early afternoon is the optimum time — and when they are fully open if you plan to serve them as a garnish. This is the best way to gather and store enough blooms in sufficient quantities to use as an ingredient if you only have one plant that is going to flower over a long period of time. Just pick a few flowers every day and keep them in the fridge whilst you build up a supply.

Remove any foliage and cut the flowers away from the stem so you are left with the head. Inspect for any insects and use a dry cloth or a small paintbrush to remove them. Do not be tempted to rinse them at this stage. Layer your flowers gently in an airtight container until you want to use them. When that time comes, if they look like they might need reviving, sit them in a shallow bowl of iced water but do not submerge them and discard any that have turned brown. Rinse and pat dry with absorbent paper before adding to food.

Freezer

Like fruits, some flowers freeze better than others. Tiny flowers such as forget-me-nots and daisies hold their shapes well when

frozen and so do the spiked florets of grape hyacinths. The large fleshy heads of camellias, roses and lilies do not withstand freezing – they quickly turn brown and mushy – but if you remove individual petals you will get better results. Freeze them flat in separate reusable plastic bags and seal. Because of their high water content most flowers tend to go soggy as they defrost, but as they look so beautiful when they are frozen it is a shame not to experiment. The best results will come from using them straight from the freezer in cold drinks or to decorate ice creams and sorbets and other frozen or chilled desserts. To make floral ice cubes and lollies see Culinary Extras, page 107.

Drying edible flowers and foliage

The best way to build up a stock of edible flowers is to dry them. Many ornamental flowers, herb flowers and foliage will keep their colour and their scent when dried. Their texture will obviously change so it's not possible to make a salad from dried flowers.

Use them as a condiment for extra seasoning and flavouring and add dried herb flowers to soups, broths, stews and casseroles. Have a jar of colourful edible petal confetti (see page 116) on the go to use for cake and cookie decorating and sprinkle across icing and frosting before it sets hard. You can also add a handful to meringue and macaroon mixtures and all kinds of custard-based desserts. One of the best ways to use dried edible foliage is in home-made teas and tisanes – the just-boiled water will revive the leaves and release their aroma.

Air drying

This is the most straightforward way to dry freshly picked flowers. Air drying is a completely natural method that encourages the natural moisture within the component parts of a flower to evaporate over time. The drying process can take a couple of days for a wispy single stem with a small head such as a cornflower or up to a few weeks for dense fleshy flowers like dahlias and sunflowers.

There is no doubt that the scent and taste of a home-made rose jam, layered between two halves of Victoria sponge and consumed on a grey January day, has the power to conjure up a Proustian moment of summer past and evoke all the pleasure of being in the garden in June.

Pick flowers when they are in full bloom. To reduce the drying time cut away any buds and as much foliage as possible without damaging the flower and keep the stems quite short.

Once picked, lay your flowers out on a flat surface and remove any excess moisture by dabbing them with absorbent paper or a soft tea towel. Remove any brown petals, traces of soil or tiny insects with a pair of tweezers.

Take a length of soft twine, fine gauge florist's wire or a reusable rubber band and secure it gently around the bare stem, leaving enough flexibility so you can easily attach it to a hook or a peg. You can combine wispy stems to make small bunches but make sure that the heads are not touching. For roses, camellias and other multi-petalled heads drying them separately produces the best results.

Suspend your flowers upside down on a hook in a dry space away from direct sunlight or bright electric light as this causes the colours to bleach. They need to be in a place where the air can circulate freely and should be kept bone dry. If they get damp, they will go mouldy and rot. If you see this happening in one bunch or even in one flower, then discard it immediately as the mould spreads very quickly to other bunches.

Once the drying process starts, the heads will droop. The stems will start to feel brittle and gradually the whole flower will follow. It is dry and ready to use when it feels papery to the touch. At this stage you can remove them from their hooks, cut off the stems and store the heads in glass jars or any other sealed container away from the light or leave them suspended ready to use in your food prep.

Drying by direct heat source

It is easy to dehydrate fresh edible flower petals and foliage by drying them rapidly via a direct heat source so they can be used in cooking weeks, months or even years after they have been picked. The key to doing this successfully it to start the drying process immediately after picking and to work in small batches. This is an efficient method for drying single leaves to make teas and tisanes or lots

of individual petals to make edible confetti.

An airing cupboard or a boiler room is the perfect environment for overnight drying but an oven on a very low heat for a couple of hours or repeated bursts of a few seconds in the microwave will produce the same results.

Spread out leaves and/or an assortment of petals that have been carefully removed from the flower head on a tray or other flat surface. Use a baking tray lined with greaseproof paper for oven drying or a plate for microwave drying. Dry them until they are slightly crispy but not totally desiccated as they will crumble too quickly when handled.

Store in recycled spice jars or vintage tins away from direct sunlight and use as required.

Pressing

Pressing the heads of edible flowers is another way to make them last. Again, they will retain their shapes and colours for up to a year if you keep them in an air-tight container and layer between sheets of tissue paper. Flat-headed flowers such as violas, pansies and primulas are the easiest to press. If you have a flower press you are ready to go; if not you can use sheets of thin card layered between two pieces of plywood and bound together with ribbon or simply place your flower heads between two layers of blotting paper and place under a heavy book. Small individual flower heads will be ready within a week and make beautiful decorations for cakes and cookies.

Preserving

There are many ways to preserve and conserve edible flowers following the same methods as fruits and vegetables (see Culinary Extras). Preserved flowers in sugar, salt, vinegar and alcohol will last for at least six months, although they will gradually start to lose their colour.

Salt, sugar and vinegar all act as preserving mediums and allow for imaginative experiments with various flowers and leaves in small batch combinations.

Alcohol is more expensive but an equally effective option. Choose a clear, unflavoured alcohol such as gin or vodka: about 250ml (1 cup) to 30g (1½ cups) of edible petals.

Place the petals in a sterilized glass jar (see page 80) and cover with the alcohol. It should roughly be the same amount of alcohol to petals. Leave to macerate in the fridge for a week and then strain into a sterilized bottle. Use for adding flavour to both sweet and savoury dishes, dilute for long drinks or enjoy as a flower-powered shot.

Edibles directory

The directory includes 100 different varieties of edible ornamental flowers also known as edimentals, herb and vegetable flowers, edible flower seeds and the best tasting flower foliage. All of them are completely safe to eat but please see the disclaimer on page 164. For anyone starting out I would recommend growing a few entries from each section so you end up with a good repertoire of ingredients and garnishes for flavouring and decorating a wide range of sweet and savoury dishes.

Ornamental flowers (edimentals)

① *ABUTILON × HYBRIDUM*
Abutilon, flowering maple

A slow growing semi-evergreen shrub with edible petals.

HEIGHT & SPREAD 2.5 × 2.5m (8 × 8ft)

GROWING Abutilons are tender shrubs that can be grown from seed in early spring or purchased as small nursery-grown plants. Grow them in a container or in a well-protected bed in full sun in moist but well-drained soil. They make perfect conservatory plants.

CARE To keep them in shape prune them back in late winter or early spring before they start to put on any new growth.

FLOWERS Showy bell-shaped flowers appear all summer long in a variety of hues ranging from peach, apricot and cream to deeper pinks and mauves depending on the variety.

HARVEST Pick the flowers for drying or use them fresh for decoration or as a garnish. Each flower has five petals that separate easily from the calyx. Only eat the petals – they have a citrussy flavour that is more easily discerned when steeped in hot water to make a tisane.

② *ALCEA ROSEA*
Hollyhock

A hardy perennial with edible petals.

HEIGHT & SPREAD 1.5 × 1.2m (5 × 4ft)

GROWING Grow from seed sown under glass in early spring or directly into a bed in late spring or autumn. Hollyhocks are prolific self-seeders once they are established. Dig up young seedlings if they become too numerous.

CARE Their foliage is prone to rust – this does not damage the plant but remove any leaves as soon as rust spots appear. Cut down the whole plant after flowering to a height of 15cm (6in).

FLOWERS Traditionally associated with cottage gardens, hollyhocks flower on tall vertical spires in a wide colour palette. The deep pinks and dark mauves look best on a plate. They flower from mid- to late summer.

HARVEST Use freshly picked flowers and separate the petals from the calyx, remove the stamen and blow away excess pollen. Use in salads, jellies and fruit-based desserts or as cake decorations for beauty rather than flavour.

③ *ALLIUM TRIQUETUM*
Snowbell, three-cornered leek

A hardy perennial with edible flowers, stems and foliage.

HEIGHT & SPREAD 30 × 20cm (12 × 8in)

GROWING Grow from bulbs planted in the autumn. Consider planting in a container if you want to restrict growth – the small bulbs multiply rapidly and can be invasive in a small space.

CARE This is a low maintenance plant that thrives in most situations. It is excellent for ground cover and suits wild areas of the garden. Dig out clumps if you see it is multiplying too rapidly.

FLOWERS The flowers resemble white bluebells with a lovely green streak running through them. They are easily discernible by their garlicky smell. They bloom from late spring to mid summer.

HARVEST Pick the flowers, stems and foliage as necessary to use in all kinds of savoury dishes – soups, stews and casseroles in lieu of garlic, spring onions, chives or leeks. You can also eat all parts of the plant raw in salads or dips. Like garlic, snowbells have beneficial health-giving properties that help to reduce blood pressure and cholesterol levels.

4 *ANCHUSA AZUREA*
Alkanet

A hardy perennial with edible flowers.

HEIGHT & SPREAD 50 × 50cm (20 × 20in)

GROWING Grow from seed sown in the autumn or spring scattered directly where you want it to appear. Alkanets will thrive in poor soil and tolerate shade. Use them as filler plants in borders or as part of a naturalistic planting scheme.

CARE They do not like to sit in water so add a light mulch to the base of the plant in autumn. Cut back to the ground after flowering to encourage bushy growth for the following year.

FLOWERS Clusters of tiny bright blue flowers will appear in early summer on stems that are slightly prickly. Wear gloves when picking flowers.

HARVEST Snip off the flower heads and store in the fridge. Use them as decorations to float in drinks, make ice cubes and lollies, or add as a garnish to salads and soft cheeses or dips.

5 *ANTIRRHINUM*
Snapdragon

A tender perennial with edible flowers.

HEIGHT & SPREAD 50 × 50cm (20 × 20in)

GROWING Snapdragons are easy to grow from seed. As tender plants they should not go into the ground until all danger of frost has passed. Start off as individual plants in pots on a windowsill. Transfer to a bed or container in a sunny spot.

CARE Pinch out new tips on young plants between your thumb and forefinger to encourage bushy new growth further down the stems.

FLOWERS If you sow a packet of seeds such as 'Sonnet Mixed' you will end up with plants in a rainbow range of colours. The pretty ruffled-edged flowers bloom successively from early to late summer. If you squeeze them by the throat they will open and shut and that is how they get their common name.

HARVEST Snip off the flower heads as they appear – this encourages more flowers. They have a slightly bitter taste and can be eaten whole but have no real flavour. Use as decoration on desserts or cakes and in long cold drinks and cocktails. They look lovely skewered alongside an olive on a cocktail stick and retain their shape and texture well when stored in the fridge.

6 BEGONIA × TUBERHYBRIDA
Begonia

A tender perennial with edible flowers.

HEIGHT & SPREAD 40 × 40cm (16 × 16in)

GROWING Grow from bulbs planted in early spring and keep under cover until you see the first signs of growth. Begonias are traditionally grown as bedding plants and are a favourite for hanging baskets. They are generally treated as annuals and regarded as old-fashioned but grow them as perennials for eating and they serve a whole new purpose.

CARE Lift the bulbs after flowering before the first frosts appear, cut away any growth and store in a warm, dry space until the following spring. If they are in pots bring them under cover and allow to die back. Remove spent flowers.

FLOWERS Begonias have been bred to flower in a wide array of colours with both single and double-headed varieties on offer, some with trailing tendencies. Mix them up for a joyful display both in the garden and on the plate. They will flower all summer long.

HARVEST Snip off the flowers from the parent plant with small scissors and add to summer salads and dips or soft cheeses. They have a crisp, crunchy texture similar to cucumber.

7 BELLIS PERENNIS
Common daisy

A hardy perennial with edible flowers and foliage.

HEIGHT & SPREAD 10 × 10cm (4 × 4in)

GROWING Although considered a weed by many gardeners, daisies are to be encouraged for attracting pollinating insects. If you see them popping up unwanted in your lawn simply dig them up and move them somewhere else. Otherwise, grow from seed and sow direct wherever you want them to appear. They look wonderful in a naturalistic setting or a wildflower meadow.

CARE No real maintenance is required. They will come back year after year with a tendency to self-seed in nooks and crannies.

FLOWERS Easy to recognize, the tiny flowers with yellow centres and white petals that sometimes take on a pinkish tinge appear on mounds of green foliage all summer.

HARVEST Pick the leaves when they are still young as they tend to get bitter over time and add to salads or cook in stir-fries. The flowers can be picked at any time – they add texture to any dish but have no real flavour. Scatter them over stir-fries, omelettes and fritattas. Do not pick daisies for eating from the kerbside or any other location where there is a risk of pollution.

8 CALENDULA
Pot marigold, English marigold

A hardy annual with edible petals and leaves (see page 37).

HEIGHT & SPREAD 50 × 50cm (20 × 20in)

GROWING Grow from seed sown in early spring or the previous autumn. Best results are achieved from scattering seed directly into the ground. Autumn sown seedlings will continue to put on growth even if it gets very cold.

CARE Pinching out the tops of fresh green tips will encourage bushy growth. Allow some plants to set seed after flowering and then disperse to come back the following year.

FLOWERS There are many varieties of *calendula* ranging in colours from buttery yellows to soft peaches. All are edible but for the greatest impact on the plate, the bright orange flowers are the most striking and hold and impart their colour well when dried.

HARVEST If your garden is well protected or you have a greenhouse it is possible to have calendula plants in flower for most of the year. Pick them as required and use fresh or dried as an alternative to saffron for colouring rice-based dishes, or use the flower heads to make a tea and strain before drinking. The leaves can be used in stews, casseroles and stir-fries and added to salads. They are highly aromatic.

9 CAMELLIA JAPONICA
Common camellia, Japanese rose

An evergreen shrub with edible flowers.

HEIGHT & SPREAD 2.5 × 4m (8 × 13ft)

GROWING Buy as a small specimen and plant according to the instructions. Camellias prefer acidic soil and are perfect for woodland conditions. If your soil is more alkaline, then grow them in a pot filled with acidic compost.

CARE Camellias like to be in shade or partial shade and should be protected from harsh winds and direct sunlight as the buds and flowers damage easily, turn brown and drop off. Do not eat these. Plants growing in the ground will not require watering but check that those in pots do not dry out. Prune lightly after flowering to keep them in shape.

FLOWERS One of the earliest shrubs to put on a show in late winter/early spring the beautiful rose-shaped blooms appear at the end of glossy-leaved branchlets. They are a cheering sight when there a few other flowers in the garden and so worth growing.

HARVEST As a close relation to the tea plant (*Camellia sinensis*) the flower heads make refreshing tisanes with a sweet fruity flavour. Alternatively, use the petals to scatter across cakes and desserts.

10 CAMPANULA PERSICIFOLIA
Peach-leaved bellflower

A hardy perennial with edible flowers.

HEIGHT & SPREAD 90 × 50cm (36 × 20in)

GROWING Grow from seed or as plug plants in well-drained soil in an open sunny spot. Campanulas look lovely in a naturalistic setting and can be easily incorporated into wildflower schemes.

CARE Once established the plants are low maintenance although they may require staking if they get too tall. Allow for self-seeding to establish a good colony of plants.

FLOWERS The pretty bell-shaped flowers will bloom all summer long. They tend to be bright blue in colour but will sometimes veer towards lilac, pale pink or white.

HARVEST Pick the flowers as they appear, detach gently from the main stem and consume them fresh. They will keep in the fridge for several days. They have a mild bland taste and can be used in both sweet and savoury dishes. They look stunning as decorations and garnishes. Toss in a salad or combine in vegetable dips.

11 CELOSIA ARGENTEA
Cock's comb, wool flower

A half-hardy annual with edible flowers, leaves and stems.

HEIGHT & SPREAD 40 × 30cm (16 × 12in)

GROWING Grow from seed sown under cover in early spring and transplant outdoors when all danger of frost has passed. Grows well in containers.

CARE Plant in full sun and keep soil moist. If you see rust spots on any leaves remove them immediately. They will flower from early to late summer.

FLOWERS The striking plume-shaped flowers are known as infloresences. What looks like the main flower is made up of a cluster of tiny individual flowers and resembles the feathers on a cockerel, hence its common name. Find them in a range of strong vibrant colours.

HARVEST Pick the infloresences when they are young and tender. Harvest leaves and stems at the same time but do not strip completely – treat it as a cut-and-come again plant. Boil or steam as a vegetable like spinach or broccoli – cooking should be minimal to retain the colours. Drizzle with olive oil and season to eat as a side dish or add to stews and casseroles. The whole plant is rich in vitamin E and folic acid.

12 CENTAUREA CYANUS
Cornflower

A hardy annual with edible flowers.

HEIGHT & SPREAD 50 × 50cm (20 × 20in)

GROWING Grow from seed sown directly where you want them to appear in autumn or spring. The seeds are tiny so sprinkle sparingly and thin out after germination if necessary. They are beautiful as part of a wildflower meadow.

CARE Cornflowers are very easy to grow and require little maintenance. They will flower all summer and like full sun.

FLOWERS The bright blue heads of cornflowers are the most commonly grown but they also come in pink, purple and white. Each single flower sits on top of a wispy stem and they are perfect for drying very quickly.

HARVEST Pick flowers as they arrive. They can be stored in the fridge to use as pops of colour on salads. The best way to use them is to dry them on the stem suspended upside-down in bunches. Once dry, cut off the delicate heads with a sharp pair of scissors and combine with other dried edible petals and small flower heads to make a colourful petal confetti for decorating cakes – especially wedding cakes. Their flavour is negligible, but they look very pretty and crystallize well.

13 CHRYSANTHEMUM CORONARIUM
Chrysanthemum, crown daisy

A tender perennial with edible flowers and leaves.

HEIGHT & SPREAD 60 × 60cm (24 × 24in)

GROWING Purchase as small pot plants in early summer and transplant into a bed or a large container. They will put on plenty of bushy growth before flowering.

CARE Cut back to ground level after flowering. They are easy plants to propagate, and you can create lots of new plants from one parent plant. Uncover some of the soil to reveal rooted stems. Pull them away gently and transfer to a small pot of compost.

FLOWERS All chrysanthemums are edible, but the variety most often grown for eating is 'coronarium', a double yellow form with a daisy-like head. The flowers appear in autumn.

HARVEST The petals and whole flower heads, fresh or dried, can be used in tisanes and bouillons, broths and soups. They are extremely aromatic with strong anti-inflammatory properties and are earthy and herby in taste. The leaves are a staple in Asian cuisine and can be steamed or stir-fried in sesame oil and seasoned with soya sauce.

14 *COSMOS SULPHUREUS*
Sulphur cosmos

A half-hardy annual with edible flowers and leaves.

NOTE *This is the only variety of cosmos that is safe to eat.*

HEIGHT & SPREAD 50 × 50cm (20 × 20in)

GROWING Grow from seed sown in early spring scattered directly where you want them to grow. Thin out seedlings as necessary to create space.

CARE Cosmos like to be in full sun and require well-drained soil. They will start to die back if their roots become waterlogged. They flower all summer long and regular picking will encourage new growth. Do not allow the flowers to set seed until the end of the season as this will prevent further flowering.

FLOWERS Sulphur cosmos come in a range of bright orange, red and yellow flowers with daisy-like heads, popular with pollinating insects.

HARVEST The flowers can be used in many seasonal fruit and vegetable dishes for zest and colour – scatter over a ratatouille or combine with fruit-based desserts such as poached peaches. Due to their long flowering time there will be regular quantities for picking. Combine the foliage with other salad and herb leaves and dress with lemon juice and olive oil.

15 *DAHLIA*
Dahlia

A tender perennial with edible petals and tubers.

HEIGHT & SPREAD up to 90cm × up to 30cm (36 × 12in) depending on variety

GROWING Grow from tubers potted up in the spring. As soon as you see green shoots appear and all danger of frost has passed, plant them outside in a sunny sheltered spot.

CARE Dahlias are tender and will not survive freezing temperatures. Lift the tubers in the autumn when the flowers have finished. Let them dry out and wrap in hessian or newspaper for repotting the following year. Tall varieties need staking.

FLOWERS There are hundreds of different types of dahlias bearing flowers in a multitude of shapes, sizes and colours, from simple daisy-like heads to elaborate ruffles and spikes. Petals from all flower types are edible. They put on a wonderful show from mid- to late summer.

HARVEST The tubers are eaten widely in South America and treated like a potato. Petals can be used in many sweet and savoury dishes. Flavours vary according to variety and resemble different fruits and vegetables. They are crunchy and refreshing in texture and delicious. Gently remove individual petals from the main flower head before eating.

16 DIANTHUS
Pink, carnation, sweet william

A hardy perennial with edible flowers (see page 41).

HEIGHT & SPREAD 30 × 20cm (12 × 8in)

GROWING Grow from seed sown under cover in the spring or purchase as plug plants for potting on. To see them in detail, plant at the front of a border as edging plants or in small pots.

CARE Dianthus thrive in sunny spots in well-drained soil. If growing in pots use grit as a top dressing to provide extra drainage so they never sit with their roots in water.

FLOWERS Highly scented flowers will appear from mid- to late summer. They are extremely pretty and come in a range of primary and pastel shades, often with a frilly two-tone edging. To add to their good looks, their unique scent and taste make them an invaluable addition to an edible flower garden.

HARVEST Snip the flowers off with sharp scissors as they appear. The have a sweet spicy taste with an underlying hint of cloves. Use to make sugar syrups or floral sugars and combine in cake, cookie and pancake batters or add to ice creams and sorbets. They also look stunning served fresh or dried as decoration on meringues and macaroons.

17 FORSYTHIA × INTERMEDIA
Forsythia, golden bells

A fast-growing deciduous shrub with edible flowers.

HEIGHT & SPREAD 2.5 × 2.5m (8 × 8ft)

GROWING Plant as a small specimen purchased from a nursery or garden centre in autumn or early spring. In a small space you can train a forsythia to grow against a wall in an attractive fan shape.

CARE After flowering, cut back old stems at the base of the plant to encourage new growth. Trim flower shoots back to new buds to keep it in shape.

FLOWERS Masses of little golden tubular-shaped flowers appear in spring all along the branches. The exact shade of yellow will depend on the variety but all bring a cheerful accent of joy in spring and will keep coming for about a month.

HARVEST Pick flowers in quantities to use for infusing honey or to make jellies. They can be eaten raw with early spring vegetables and look fabulous scattered over a plate of steamed asparagus. They can also be used to make teas – use a handful of flowers to make a tisane and leave to steep or layer between black or brown tea leaves for a conventional brew.

18 *FREESIA*
Freesia

A tender perennial with edible flowers.

HEIGHT & SPREAD 25 × 15cm (10 × 6in)

GROWING Grow from corms planted under cover in spring. When you see the first signs of green shoots they can be transplanted outside provided all danger of frost has passed.

CARE Freesias like full sun and very well-drained soil. Add grit if necessary to the planting hole. They grow well in containers. Leave the foliage to die back after flowering has finished and lift the corms in the autumn to store in a dry place before replanting the following spring.

FLOWERS Delicate arching sprays of highly scented flowers in a rainbow range of colours appear in late spring and early summer. Picking the flowers regularly will encourage more to come.

HARVEST Pick the whole stem with the flowers intact and crystallize for extra special decorations on cakes. Single flowers can then be broken off and eaten individually. Alternatively, harness their amazing perfume by making sugars and syrups or serve as a garnish and consume raw.

19 *FUCHSIA*
Fuchsia

A hardy shrub with edible flowers.

HEIGHT & SPREAD 1.1 × 1.1m (3¼ × 3¼ft)

GROWING Purchase in autumn or spring as a small plant from a garden centre or nursery and transfer to a bed or a large container. Although they are quite exotic in appearance, fuchsias will tolerate partial shade and bring a pop of colour to a dark corner. They need to be protected from wind as the flowers are easily damaged.

CARE Most varieties are very fast growing. Cut back after flowering to keep them neat, especially if they are in a container.

FLOWERS From May to October fuchsias put on a wonderful showy display of two-toned pendant-like flowers in scarlets and purples. Other subtler varieties come in pale pinks but for the purposes of eating – the more vibrant the better.

HARVEST Pick the flowers with a sharp pair of scissors and use for crystallizing or in jellies. They are juicy but the taste is slightly bitter so coating them in sugar makes them more palatable. Alternatively use them in salads or as a decorative garnish. Remove the long pistils before eating.

20 *GALIUM ODORATUM*
Sweet woodruff

A hardy perennial with edible flowers.

HEIGHT & SPREAD 20 × 35cm (8 × 15in)

GROWING Grow from seed scattered in the autumn or early spring directly where you want it to appear. Sweet woodruff is one of the best plants for evergreen ground cover, especially in shady areas, and is perfect for growing under trees, shrubs and bulbs. It spreads very quickly by forming rhizomes underground.

CARE This is a very self-sufficient plant. As it spreads you can easily dig out small clumps to plant elsewhere. Cut back any browning foliage in the autumn.

FLOWERS Tiny white star-shaped flowers first appear in early spring and continue to arrive until early summer. They are sweetly scented and are very attractive to pollinating insects.

HARVEST Snip off the tiny flowers to use fresh or dry them and store in an airtight tin. They have an underlying taste of vanilla and are traditionally used to steep in white wine, but you can also use them for vinegars and syrups or scatter them over cakes and desserts.

21 GARDENIA JASMINOIDES
Cape jasmine

A semi-hardy evergreen shrub with edible flowers.

HEIGHT & SPREAD 90 × 90cm (36 × 36in)

GROWING Purchase as a small plant and transfer to a bed or container. Gardenias prefer acidic soil and need to be in a warm sheltered position in dappled shade away from bright sunlight. Also grown as house plants.

CARE Low maintenance but they should be watered with rainwater and not tap water. The glossy evergreen leaves can be wiped with a soft damp cloth if they start to gather dust indoors. They will survive a frost outside but if you are growing them in a pot, bring them indoors if there is a prolonged period of cold weather.

FLOWERS The single white rosette-shaped flowers are waxy in texture and their perfume is intoxicating. Outside they appear successively throughout the summer but indoors the flowering period will continue until the winter.

HARVEST Pick the flowers as they appear. They are intensely sweet with an almond-like flavour. Use them for floral sugars and syrups, turn them into jams and jellies or infuse whole into honey. They make a delicious tea or cordial. A few flowers go a long way.

22 GLADIOLUS COMMUNIS
Gladioli, sword lily

A hardy perennial with edible flowers.

HEIGHT & SPREAD 90 × 90cm (36 × 36in)

GROWING Grow from corms planted directly into the ground or in a container in late spring. They need a hole of at least 10cm (4in) to keep them stable. Stagger the planting over a few weeks to prolong the flowering period. Plant against a wall or fence to provide support.

CARE Hardy gladioli corms can be left to overwinter *in situ* but if you are gardening in clay soil that gets very waterlogged it is advisable to lift the corms.

FLOWERS From early summer the tall vertical stems start to produce spikes of foliage followed by large funnel-shaped flowers that appear gradually to create accents of colour. Flowering starts at the bottom of each spike and gradually reaches the top. Choose the colour according to variety.

HARVEST Cut the flowers off from the main spike – do not wait for the whole plant to flower as this happens consecutively and do not cut off the main spike. Store picked flowers in the fridge for several days. Their shape makes them ideal for stuffing, and they can be used in lieu of small bowls for dips and spreads. Remove the anthers first. They have a mild taste similar to lettuce.

23 HELIANTHUS ANNUUS
Sunflower

A hardy annual with edible flower buds, petals and seeds (see page 69).

HEIGHT & SPREAD 1m × 40cm (39 × 16in)

GROWING Sow from seed into pots or directly into the ground in late spring or under cover in autumn. Choose a sunny open spot if sowing direct and space the seeds at least 40cm (16in) apart. Alternatively, grow single plants in large containers.

CARE Sunflowers only require minimal watering. Taller varieties may need staking, especially if they are in containers.

FLOWERS The brightly coloured happy faces of sunflowers make them a joy to grow. If the bright yellow flowers are too much of a statement, then choose more subtle tones to suit your planting scheme. Flowers will arrive from midsummer onwards.

HARVEST Remove the petals but leave the flower head on the plant. Use the petals fresh with vegetable dishes and salads or dry them. Allow the seed head to ripen before removing it to retrieve the edible seeds. You can also eat the fleshy flower buds of sunflowers – pick them before the petals arrive and treat them like an artichoke.

㉔ *HEMEROCALLIS*
Day lily

A hardy perennial with edible buds and flowers.

HEIGHT & SPREAD 65 × 60cm (26 × 24in)

GROWING Grow from tubers planted in the autumn or spring. Plant in a sunny well-drained spot in an open bed or in a large container.

CARE Day lilies are very robust and largely self-sufficient plants that require little looking after. Water young plants to ensure they do not dry out. Cut back to ground level after flowering has finished. The plants are easy to divide after a couple of years.

FLOWERS Large trumpet-shaped flowers will appear each day for about a month in midsummer in rich fiery hues depending on the variety. They are not true lily flowers but named because of their shape.

HARVEST Pick the flowers as they arrive. Daily picking will encourage more to come. You can eat them fresh – they are easy to stuff with cream cheese and puréed vegetables, or cook them in a light batter. Remove the anthers first. The young buds can be steamed and dressed with olive oil or butter and have a similar taste to green beans. You can also break the petals gently away from the flower head to eat separately.

㉕ *HIBISCUS SYRIACUS*
Rose of Sharon

A hardy perennial shrub with edible petals (see page 49).

HEIGHT & SPREAD 2.5m × 70cm (8ft × 27in)

GROWING Buy as a small plant from a nursery or garden centre and plant in full sun in well-drained soil. You can also grow hibiscus in containers – look out for dwarf varieties.

CARE Prune back lightly in the spring before flowering to encourage a bushy shape. Do not allow container grown plants to dry out.

FLOWERS Hibiscus flowers are easily recognizable for the large protruding stamen at their centre. They appear from mid-late summer until early autumn and they open and close with the sun. They range in colour from whites and pale pinks to dark reds and mauves. For edible purposes the darker varieties are the best choice.

HARVEST Pick the flowers when they are in full bloom in the middle of the day with a pair of sharp scissors. Separate the petals from the calyx and discard the stamen. The petals can be consumed fresh but best results are obtained from drying them. They have an intense fruity flavour. Use for tisanes, syrups and cordials and add to fruit-based dishes, jellies, sorbets and ice creams.

26 IBERIS UMBELLATA
Candytuft

A half-hardy annual with edible flowers.

HEIGHT & SPREAD 25 × 25cm (10 × 10in)

GROWING Grow from seed directly sown in the spring. Candytuft thrives in poor soil and makes good ground cover.

CARE The plants are tough and drought tolerant requiring little maintenance.

FLOWERS Small florets of pink, white and purple flowers appear from midsummer to autumn. Each floret is made of up of tiny individual flowers.

HARVEST Pick the flowers as they appear. They can be broken up for scattering across salads and vegetable dishes, floated in drinks, used in dips or as a garnish. They are members of the brassica/mustard family and taste like honey-coated broccoli.

27 IMPATIENS
Busy lizzie

A tender perennial with edible flowers.

HEIGHT & SPREAD 25 × 25cm (10 × 10in)

GROWING Grow from seed sown under cover in early spring or from small plug plants. Do not plant outside until all danger of frost has passed. Outdoors they will flower all summer and then die; however, you can grow them indoors as house plants. They are happy in partial shade.

CARE Busy lizzies are perfect for pots, containers and hanging baskets but need regular watering. Their foliage can be prone to mildew so remove any damaged leaves immediately to prevent spreading.

FLOWERS Outdoor plants will flower prolifically from early summer through to the first frosts. Indoors the flowering period will be more prolonged. You can buy seeds in mixed colours – generally in pink, red, orange and white or stick to single hues. They appear in clusters with dainty open heads made up of five petals.

HARVEST Harvest all summer long. They are sweet in flavour and lend themselves well to crystallization. They can also be used in butters and soft cheeses, coated in chocolate and added to cake, shortbread and cookie recipes or floated in drinks.

28 JASMINIUM OFFICINALE
Common white jasmine

A perennial climber with edible flowers (see page 53).

HEIGHT & SPREAD 8 × 5.5m (26 × 18ft)

GROWING Grow from small plants purchased from a garden centre or nursery. As a climbing plant it is not self-supporting and needs to be trained against a trellis, wall or fence. Alternatively, let it scramble through a tree. Jasmine needs to be in full sun to flower profusely.

CARE Left to its own devices, jasmine will romp away and put on new growth quite happily year after year. Prune back after flowering has finished if it is becoming unwieldy.

FLOWERS Tiny white star-shaped flowers appear with the heat all summer long. They are intensely perfumed, and their scent is particularly strong at night.

HARVEST Snip off individual flowers with small scissors. To harness the perfume, use in floral sugars, syrups, cordials and teas. Eat the flowers raw scattered over stir-fries or steam with rice; they have a musky flavour.

29 LAVANDULA
Lavender

A hardy perennial with edible flowers (See page 57).

HEIGHT & SPREAD 60 × 75cm (24 × 30in)

GROWING Grow from small plants. There are many varieties of lavender so choose the best one to suit your space or create a mini lavender garden. They are extremely drought tolerant and thrive in poor soil but do require plenty of sun.

CARE Once flowering has finished cut back the green stems to the point at which they become woody. This may not be obvious in the first year so just cut off the longer stems to where the foliage is bushy. Don't cut into the woody stems as the plant matures as this is the easiest way to kill it.

FLOWERS Tall spikes of mainly purple, lilac or deep mauve flowers will appear throughout the summer. You can also find white varieties. English lavender will flower earlier than other cultivars. All are strongly aromatic and slightly astringent.

HARVEST Snip flowers for immediate use in syrups, floral sugars, cordials, waters and custards or to decorate and flavour cakes, cookies and shortbreads. Cut long stems for drying and hang in bunches. Leave suspended away from direct sunlight or crumble the heads into a spice jar.

30 LOBULARIA MARITIMA
Sweet alyssum

A half-hardy annual with edible flowers.

HEIGHT & SPREAD 10 × 25cm (4 × 10in)

GROWING Sow from seed scattered directly into the ground in late spring. Alyssum require full sun but are not fussy about soil type and their self-seeding habit will see them growing in nooks and crannies or wherever they can get a foothold. It is a good plant for temporary ground cover with a tendency to spread between other plants.

CARE Alyssum are drought tolerant and as their botanical name suggests, they thrive in coastal gardens where salt can be a problem for other plants. They require little maintenance.

FLOWERS Clusters of low-growing fragrant white or pink flowers appear from early summer through until the autumn.

HARVEST You will have plenty of flowers to pick so use them in ice cubes or for flavouring cold summer soups and gazpachos. They are related to the mustard/cabbage family but have a sweeter flavour. Add to potato salads, vegetable dishes, omelettes and frittatas.

31 LONICERA
Climbing honeysuckle

A perennial climber with edible flowers.

HEIGHT & SPREAD 7 × 1m (23ft × 39in)

GROWING Honeysuckles can be deciduous or evergreen depending on the variety. Plant deciduous types in winter and evergreens in spring. Buy as small plants and follow instructions for planting. Site in partial shade against a wall or fence with a support structure in place. They will grow rapidly.

CARE Cut back after flowering to keep the plant in shape. You can shear it back to its base if it becomes too leggy and new shoots will appear. Honeysuckles are prone to mildew and mulching around the base of the plant in spring will help prevent this.

FLOWERS Clusters of pretty tubular flowers will appear from late spring. They come in yellow, white, red and pink depending on the variety. For eating, select one that is strongly fragranced.

HARVEST Pick the flowers when in full bloom. To harness the fragrance use them immediately in floral sugars, jams, syrups, sorbets and ice creams or make vinegars and cordials. You can dry honeysuckle. An individual cluster makes a beautiful decoration for a celebration cake.

32 MALVA MOSCHATA
Musk mallow

A hardy perennial with edible petals.

HEIGHT & SPREAD 70 × 40cm (27 × 16in)

GROWING Grow from seed sown under cover in early spring or sow direct into the ground in late spring. Transplant seedlings into a sunny spot. This type of mallow is easy to grow and works well in a wildflower garden or a naturalized setting. It thrives in poor soil conditions.

CARE It is a prolific self-seeder so remove young plants as you see them germinate in early spring if it is becoming too invasive. It will die back completely in winter.

FLOWERS Pretty saucer-shaped flowers appear all summer long in shades of pale pink. As its name suggests, they have a sweet, slightly musky scent to them.

HARVEST Pick the flowers in full bloom and remove the petals for immediate use as a garnish or decoration. Use fresh or dried for tisanes or for making floral sugars, cordials and vinegars.

33 MONARDA
Bee balm, bergamot

A hardy perennial with edible petals.

HEIGHT & SPREAD 90 × 45cm (36 × 18in)

GROWING Grow from seed or as small plug plants. They are fussy and prefer constant moist soil that does not get too wet or too dry so good drainage is key. Add some grit to the planting hole.

CARE Monardas are prone to powdery mildew and this is best dealt with by mulching with organic matter in early spring just as they put on early growth. Pinch out the tips of the top few flowers to create bushy stems further down the plant.

FLOWERS Spiky flower bracts keep coming all summer in shades of pink, deep scarlet, white and mauve depending on the variety. They have an aromatic scent and contain oil of bergamot. Although they are not used in the commercial production of Earl Grey tea, their perfume is similar.

HARVEST Pick flowers for using fresh or dried. To make your own scented tea, layer petals between green or black tea leaves. Keep dry petals in an airtight jar to use throughout the winter for flavouring poached fruit dishes – they pair well with plums and pears. Use fresh petals for making syrups and cordials, custards and cream-based desserts.

㉞ *MUSCARI ARMENIACUM*
Grape hyacinth

A hardy perennial with edible flowers.

HEIGHT & SPREAD 20 × 50cm (8 × 20in)

GROWING Grow from bulbs planted in the autumn at a depth of 10cm (4in). Plant closely together for a tight cluster of flowers. Grape hyacinths look wonderful in pots and containers but make sure to include plenty of grit mixed in with the compost as they prefer well-drained soil. You can grow them indoors as house plants in a cool position.

CARE The tiny bulbs will multiply very quickly – for this reason they are good for naturalized settings where they can grow in swathes. If you see groups becoming too congested, lift them in the autumn to divide up the bulbs and plant elsewhere.

FLOWERS Throughout the spring, conical spikes of tiny flower heads will appear on thin green stems. The flowers come in different shades of blue and white depending on the variety.

HARVEST Snip the flower heads off once they arrive. They will keep well in the fridge and are one of the few edible flowers not to turn mushy after freezing. The have a mild onion flavour so use them in soups, broths or stews or any other type of savoury dish.

㉟ *MYOSOTIS SYLVATICA*
Forget-me-not

A short-lived perennial with edible flowers.

HEIGHT & SPREAD 30 × 15cm (12 × 6in)

GROWING Grow from seed scattered directly wherever you want it to grow. Forget-me-nots make fantastic ground cover but also look beautiful when planted in pots as a foil for tulips. They thrive in poor soil and will self-seed into walls, nooks and crannies.

CARE They will take care of themselves and require little maintenance. Any large, self-formed clumps are easy to split and divide in the autumn.

FLOWERS Tiny bright blue clusters of flowers arrive as a true arbiter of spring, putting on a show that lasts for several weeks.

HARVEST Pick them for decoration more than flavour – they look lovely on cupcakes and cookies or float them in drinks. They keep well in the fridge and can be frozen in floral ice cubes or lollies.

36 *NEPETA GRANDIFLORA*
Catmint

A hardy perennial with edible flowers and leaves.

HEIGHT & SPREAD 90 × 60cm (36 × 24in)

GROWING Grow from small plug plants purchased from a nursery or garden centre in late spring. They will soon put on plenty of vigorous bushy growth to form dense mounds that look good dotted throughout herbaceous beds or as edging plants. They like a sunny spot.

CARE In the autumn you can cut back plants to ground level.

FLOWERS Clusters of tubular-shaped flowers in shades of lavender and lilac will arrive throughout midsummer. Both the leaves and flowers are distinctly aromatic.

HARVEST Cut the stems from the base of the plant to include flowers and foliage. String up bunches for drying. Catmint is mainly used for making tisanes – you can use both the leaves and the flowers to steep in just boiled water. It has a mild minty flavour and is said to help with insomnia. Alternatively, use in the same way as a herb in cooked dishes.

37 *OENOTHERA BIENNIS*
Evening primrose

A short-lived perennial with edible petals.

HEIGHT & SPREAD 100 × 60cm (39 × 24in)

GROWING Grow from seed scattered in the autumn or spring directly where you want it to grow. Evening primrose flowers look wonderful as part of a naturalistic or wildflower planting scheme. They thrive in poor soil and will tolerate partial shade.

CARE Little care is required. Allow plants to self-seed to guarantee future flowers.

FLOWERS Blooms arrive throughout the summer months, appearing at dusk and fading at dawn. At first, they are pale yellow in colour but as the plant ages they turn more golden. The flowers are highly perfumed and attractive to night-time pollinators, particularly moths.

HARVEST Pick the flower heads in the evening as they bloom. Separate the petals from the calyx and use fresh in syrups, vinegars, floral sugars and cordials or as a decorative garnish on fruit salads. They are sweet in flavour, tasting like honey.

38 OSTEOSPERMUM
African daisy

A tender perennial with edible petals.

HEIGHT & SPREAD 40 × 40cm (16 × 16in)

GROWING Grow as small plug plants purchased from a nursery or garden centre. Do not plant out until all danger of frost has passed. These daisies need to be in full sun in a well-protected position. They are good in pots where they can be moved around and brought indoors to be grown as house plants in winter.

CARE Because they are very tender African daisies will not survive outside in winter in the colder months. They will need lifting to be brought under cover if they are growing in a bed.

FLOWERS Large daisy-shaped flowers appear throughout the summer. They tend to open and close with the sun. They are available in a wide range of vibrant colours, usually two-tone with a darker centre.

HARVEST Snip off the flower heads and gently separate the petals from the centre of the flower. They have no discernible flavour but can be used in ice cubes and lollies or as a garnish. You can also dry the petals to add to an edible confetti mix.

39 PAEONIA
Peony

A hardy perennial with edible petals.

HEIGHT & SPREAD depends on variety.

GROWING Invest in a well-established plant. Young peonies do not flower for several years. Plant just below the soil surface – too deep and they will not flower. They prefer free draining soil in a sunny spot. For growing in pots look for intersectional peonies.

CARE Once established, peonies are easy to look after. Cut back the foliage to the ground in the autumn. Tall varieties may need staking.

FLOWERS There are hundreds of varieties to choose from. They flower mainly as large bowl-shaped blooms in a range of hues from whites, lemons and pale pastel pinks to deep dark velvety crimsons. They have a sweet/spicy fragrance.

HARVEST Pick one flower at a time – the petals go a long way. Their clove-like taste can be harnessed for both sweet and savoury recipes. Treat them like rose petals to make scented waters or cordials, consume fresh with vegetables and salads or steam gently to add to rice and noodles. Larger petals make a scoop for dips or as a base for presenting ice creams. Add to oils and vinegar or use in floral sugars or coat in chocolate.

40 PASSIFLORA
Passion flower vine

A semi-evergreen climber with edible flowers.

HEIGHT & SPREAD 7 × 3m (23 × 10ft)

GROWING Buy as a small plant purchased from a nursery or garden centre. Plant in a sheltered, well-protected spot outdoors or cultivate as a conservatory plant in a large container. Train against a support and tie in the strongest shoots – tendrils will then appear to promote rapid new growth.

CARE The leaves will drop in winter, and this is the time to cut back if the plant is becoming too unwieldy.

FLOWERS The large purple or white flowers are exotic in appearance with a light lemony scent. Flowering starts in midsummer and continues until autumn. They will go on to form fruits, but these are not edible. Passion fruits available in supermarkets are grown commercially in the tropics and imported.

HARVEST Pick the flowers as they appear and gently remove the pistils, stamen and sepals with your fingers. The flowers can be eaten whole as a garnish for salads; they are crunchy in texture and impart a citrusy freshness.

41 *PHLOX PANICULATA*
Phlox

A hardy perennial with edible flowers.

HEIGHT & SPREAD 40 × 40cm (16 × 16in)

GROWING Grow from seed scattered in spring where you want it to grow or from small plug plants transferred to a sunny border. The plants are clump forming and will provide blocks of bright colour.

CARE If plants become too big for their space they can be easily divided in the autumn. Some varieties are prone to mildew and benefit from mulching in the spring.

FLOWERS Different varieties of phlox come in white, pink and red hues with clusters of small open rosette-shaped flowers that appear in midsummer. They are highly scented with a very sweet-smelling perfume.

HARVEST Many flowers will appear at the same time – snip them off as required and use in all manner of sweet recipes. They crystallize well and this is the best way to preserve them. Use for floral sugars and syrups, custards and creams, float in drinks or make ice cubes and lollies.

42 *PRIMULA VULGARIS*
Primrose

A hardy perennial with edible flowers.

HEIGHT & SPREAD 10 × 10cm (4 × 4in)

GROWING Grow from seed started off under cover in the autumn or as plug plants purchased in early spring. You can grow primroses in pots or plant them at the front of borders, so they are not dwarfed by taller plants.

CARE Plants grown in the ground will spread to form a mat of clumps over time. These can be divided to make new separate plants in the autumn when flowering has finished.

FLOWERS Small, easy to recognize flower rosettes in a pale yellow will appear in early spring.

HARVEST Snip off the flower heads once they have fully opened. They are mildly sweet in taste and can be used in both sweet and savoury foods. They look particularly lovely on omelettes and other egg-based dishes. They also crystallize beautifully and this is the best way to preserve them.

43 *ROSA*
Rose

A hardy shrub with edible flowers (see page 65).

HEIGHT & SPREAD Depends on the variety

GROWING No garden is complete without at least one rose. Choose a variety to suit your space and ensure that it is scented. Buy from a specialist rose grower and purchase in autumn as a bare root plant with no foliage or in spring when it will come in a pot. Follow the planting instructions.

CARE Roses are easy to care for and as tough as old boots. Prune back in late autumn or early spring. If you see white or greenfly on young shoots, remove them with a solution of washing-up liquid. Do not spray roses with chemicals if you wish to eat them.

HARVEST Some varieties flower for months whilst others only a few weeks. Pick flowers as they appear and consume fresh or dry. Individual petals and small flower heads dry easily. Large blowsy flower heads are difficult to dry successfully so pick them when they are still in bud and hang upside down. Almost anything can be enhanced with a hint of rose. Make jams, jellies, waters, cordials and syrups to flavour both sweet and savoury foods. Trim off the yellow heel on fresh petals before eating.

44 *SALVIA MICROPHYLLA*
Baby sage

*An evergreen shrub with edible
flowers and leaves.*

HEIGHT & SPREAD 90 × 60cm
(36 × 24in)

GROWING Grow from plug
plants purchased from a
nursery or garden centre in the
autumn or early spring. Plant
in a sunny spot at the back of a
border or in a large container.

CARE Cut back after flowering
to encourage strong bushy
growth the following year.

FLOWERS There are many
different varieties to choose
from in a range of pinks,
purples, dark reds and mauves
as well as the 'hot lips' series
with their two-tonal petals.
They have a long flowering
period from early summer
through until the autumn and
in sheltered spots will carry on
until the winter.

HARVEST Snip off the flowers
as they appear and pick the
leaves when they are tender.
Both the leaves and flowers can
be used fresh or dry for tisanes
and added to fruit-based dishes.
They taste like blackcurrants.

45 *SAMBUCUS NIGRA*
Common elder

*A deciduous shrub with edible
flowers.*

HEIGHT & SPREAD 2.5m ×
1.25cm (8 × 4ft)

GROWING Purchase as a small
specimen from a nursery or
garden centre and plant in
spring or autumn in a sunny
spot, following the instructions
for the correct depth of planting
hole and required space for the
roots.

CARE Elders will benefit from
a light mulch in autumn. This
is also the time to cut back any
unwieldy summer growth.

FLOWERS Standard cultivars
of elder produce flat-topped
clusters of flowers made up
from individual florets that
appear in early summer. You
can also find pink varieties
that make for a prettier display
and retain their colour when
cooked.

HARVEST Pick the large flower
heads and then snip off the
individual florets – store in the
fridge until you have sufficient
quantities for making cordials
or syrups. They will keep for up
to a week. Do not consume raw
elderflower heads. They can
be coated in batter and cooked
but they are slightly toxic when
raw so wash your hands after
picking and handling.

46 *SYRINGA VULGARIS*
Common lilac

A deciduous shrub with edible flowers.

HEIGHT & SPREAD 4 × 4m (13 × 13ft)

GROWING Purchase as a small specimen from a nursery or garden centre and plant according to the instructions in a sunny spot at the back of a border.

CARE Remove any dead flower heads around new shoots as you see them forming. Mulching in spring is beneficial to encourage fresh growth.

FLOWERS Dense clusters like small bunches of grapes appear in late spring. Each head is made of tiny florets in a recognizable lilac hue with an intense perfume. White flowering lilacs are available but these are not suitable for use in cooking as the flowers turn brown.

HARVEST Cut off the clusters and store whole in the fridge if necessary. Harness the perfume by snipping off the tiny florets to make syrups, cordials, jams and jellies. Use fresh to decorate cakes and sweet treats. Dip small clusters into melted chocolate or crystallize.

47 *TAGETES PATULA*
French marigold

A half-hardy annual with edible flowers.

HEIGHT & SPREAD 30 × 30cm (12 × 12in)

GROWING Grow from seed sown under cover in autumn or sow directly into the ground in spring. *Tagetes* look good in pots and are often grown as companion plants alongside vegetables. If planting in a border place them at the front. They like to be in full sun.

CARE Regular picking of the flowers will encourage more to come. Save your own seed at the end of the flowering period.

FLOWERS A brightly coloured show of single or double-headed daisy-like flowers will arrive throughout the summer months. Find them in shades of yellow, orange, red or brown to bring pops of joy to any space.

HARVEST Pick whole flower heads and use fresh on salads and vegetable dishes, granola or grains such as couscous or quinoa. They have a citrusy flavour. You can store them in the fridge. Separate the petals gently for drying to use over the winter.

48 *TARAXACUM OFFICINALE*
Dandelion

A hardy perennial with edible petals and leaves.

HEIGHT & SPREAD 10 × 10cm (4 × 4in)

GROWING Considered a weed by many gardeners, dandelions attract pollinating insects and are of huge benefit to wildlife. Grow them from seed as part of a naturalistic planting scheme and at the outer edges of borders.

CARE No care is required – they have long tap roots that find moisture underground. If you want to restrict their spread, cut off the clock-like seed heads that are easily dispersed by the wind.

FLOWERS Bright yellow flowers open during the day and shut at night from spring until autumn.

HARVEST Pick flowers and leaves when young. The leaves can be used in salads and vegetable dishes and taste a bit like rocket. Pull the petals gently away from the flower head and use to scatter over salads or mix with other edible petals for decoration. Use whole heads to make dandelion tea. They are full of antioxidants and boost the immune system.

49 *TRIFOLIUM PRATENSE*
Red clover

A hardy perennial with edible flowers.

HEIGHT & SPREAD 50 × 50cm (20 × 20in)

GROWING Grow from seed scattered directly where you want it to grow in autumn or spring. Red clover looks wonderful as part of a naturalistic planting scheme and is often found in wildflower meadows. It thrives in poor soil and requires no special conditions. Its nectar-rich flowers are a magnet for bees.

CARE No special care is required. It will spread over time to form a mat and you can dig up new plants to transfer to other spots.

FLOWERS Clusters of round pink pom-pom-shaped flowers appear from late spring through until autumn. Each one is made up of tiny individual heads.

HARVEST Snip off the flowers as they appear. They store well in the fridge. Gently break them apart before use to scatter over salads or to use in shortbreads and biscuit recipes. They are sweet in taste but not so sugary that they can't be used in a savoury dish. They also dry well – suspend a bunch upside down for a couple of days and store in an airtight jar.

50 *TROPAEOLUM MAJUS*
Nasturtium

A hardy annual with edible flowers, leaves and seeds (see page 73).

HEIGHT & SPREAD 30 × 45cm (12 × 18in)

GROWING Grow from seed scattered directly where you want them in late spring. Germination tends to be very quick. Nasturtiums thrive in poor stony soil, but they do like to be in full sun. They are perfect for pots.

CARE No special care is required. Once germination has taken place, nasturtiums are happy to look after themselves.

FLOWERS Traditional varieties flower in hues of orange, yellow and red but look out for more subtle shades in pale pink and soft peach. You can also find trailing nasturtiums that look wonderful in pots or cascading down steps.

HARVEST Pick the flowers and leaves as required and store in the fridge or use immediately. They both have a peppery flavour and can be used in salads. The leaves can be coated in batter for a quick tempura or whizzed up to make a pesto. The flowers make a beautiful garnish for vegetable dishes such as ratatouille and can be floated on chilled soups and gazpacho or stuffed with cream cheese.

51 *TULBAGHIA VIOLACEA*
Society garlic

A frost-hardy perennial with edible flowers.

HEIGHT & SPREAD 50 × 50cm (20 × 20in)

GROWING Grow from rhizomes planted in early spring or as small plants purchased from a nursery or garden centre. Plant at the front of the border or in a pot in full sun. Add some grit to pots for extra drainage.

CARE Cut off yellowing foliage after flowering. In very exposed areas, the rhizomes should be lifted and stored under cover or potted plants can be moved into an unheated greenhouse for winter protection.

FLOWERS Umbels of beautiful lilac-coloured flowers appear from late summer through until the autumn, and are a lovely way to extend colour in the garden as other ornamentals start to fade. They have a distinct smell of garlic.

HARVEST Pick the whole flower head and gently split the umbel into separate parts. Store in the fridge and use in place of garlic, onions and chives in any manner of savoury recipes. Scatter over cooked vegetables and soups, use in omelettes and frittatas, pizza doughs and bread or to decorate and flavour soft cheeses.

52 *TULIPA*
Tulip

A perennial bulb with edible petals.

HEIGHT & SPREAD 30 × 10cm (12 × 4in)

GROWING Grow from bulbs planted in late autumn or early winter after a period of very cold weather. Plant directly into the ground or into pots. Position the bulbs close together but not touching if you want natural-looking groups.

CARE Leave foliage to turn yellow and die back before cutting away. Nutrients from the leaves feed the bulb to make next year's flowers. Lift bulbs in pots and store in a cool, dry place.

FLOWERS There are so many different varieties that it is possible to have them flowering from mid-spring through to early summer. You can also stagger the planting time of specific varieties to ensure that flowers keep coming.

HARVEST Cut off the whole stem at the base of the plant and then cut off the flower head. Gently remove the petals from the calyx and blow away any pollen. Discard the anthers. Petals can be stored in the fridge. Use as a garnish or decoration or use a large petal for consuming dips and spreads – they taste like cucumber. Trim away the yellow or white heel before eating.

53 *VIOLA*
Pansy

A hardy perennial with edible flowers.

HEIGHT & SPREAD 10 × 40cm (4 × 16in)

GROWING Grow from seed sown under cover in the autumn or outdoors in spring or as small plug plants. Look for mixed colours to create joyful displays for pots, planters and hanging baskets. Pansies will tolerate shade but take care not to let pots dry out and water regularly.

CARE Do not let seed heads form – snip them off to encourage regular flowering. In sheltered positions you can have pansies in flower all year.

FLOWERS The flowers have such cheerful faces and are worth growing for easy pops of year-round colour. The petals on each flower make a lovely heart shape. Find them in contrasting hues often with intricate markings at their centres.

HARVEST Snip off the flowers for immediate use or store them in the fridge. They have a crisp texture and a mild slightly minty flavour and work in both sweet and savoury dishes. Use them as the main ingredient for a floral salad, as decoration for cakes and desserts, and in lollies and jellies where you can see them at their best. They are also good for crystallization.

54 *VIOLA ODORATA*
Sweet violet

A hardy perennial with edible flowers.

HEIGHT & SPREAD 10 × 20cm (4 × 8in)

GROWING Grow from seed sown under cover in the autumn or sow directly where you want plants to grow in early spring. Sweet violets make wonderful ground cover – they will spread quickly to form mats of colour and are good for planting under trees and as part of a naturalistic scheme or in a wildflower garden. They are happy in shade.

CARE Little maintenance is required. Dig up clumps as they multiply and separate to plant elsewhere in the autumn.

FLOWERS Tiny flowers in an unmistakeable violet colour with a memorable scent will appear in early spring.

HARVEST Snip flowers as they arrive and store in the fridge until you have enough to make jams or syrups. A handful is plenty as they are intensely perfumed. Use as decorations in all sweet recipes and crystallize to preserve the flowers for future use.

55 *ZINNIA*
Zinnia

A half-hardy annual with edible petals.

HEIGHT & SPREAD 50 × 30cm (20 × 12in)

GROWING Grow from seed sown under cover in early spring or directly outdoors in late spring when all danger of frost has passed. Thin out seedlings if necessary. Zinnias like to be in full sun. Sow successionally over a period of weeks to extend the flowering period.

CARE Pinch out the new green tips to encourage plants to bush out. Regular watering and deadheading will keep the flowers coming.

FLOWERS From mid- to late summer zinnias will put on a show in a wide range of sweetie-shop colours. Their flat-faced tightly packed blooms are a magnet for pollinating insects.

HARVEST One flower head is sufficient for scattering over a salad or chilled soup. Gently pull away the petals from the calyx. They do not have a strong flavour but use them to add colour and crunch to summery dishes or dry them to mix with other petals for an edible confetti mix.

Herb flowers

① *AGASTACHE*
Anise hyssop

A short-lived hardy perennial with edible flowers and foliage.

HEIGHT & SPREAD 90 × 40cm (36 × 16in)

GROWING Grow from seed sown under cover in the autumn or as small plug plants purchased from a nursery or garden centre in the spring. The final planting position should be in full sun.

CARE *Agastache* hate to have their roots in water. They are extremely drought tolerant and will thrive in stony soil. Water sparingly and add grit to planting holes to improve drainage. Divide larger plants in the early spring.

FLOWERS Tall flower spikes in the shape of bottlebrushes put on a wonderful display from midsummer to early autumn mainly in colours of blues and violets. Their aromatic perfume is a magnet for bees and other pollinators.

HARVEST Cut the whole flower spike off at the base of the stem. Dry bunches suspended upside down to use throughout the winter. Crumble the leaves and flowers into soups and stews. Use them fresh in small quantities to flavour poached summer fruits or blend with cream cheese. Both the leaves and flowers have a strong liquorice flavour.

② *ALLIUM SCHOENOPRASUM*
Chive

A hardy perennial with edible flowers and foliage.

HEIGHT & SPREAD 50 × 10cm (20 × 4in)

GROWING Grow from seed sown directly where you want it in the spring. Thin out plants to a spacing of 10cm (4in) after germination. Chives are an integral plant for herb or kitchen gardens but look lovely in edible ornamental schemes. They will thrive in partial shade.

CARE Little maintenance is required. Chives will come back reliably year after year. Divide clumps in the autumn if they become too big.

FLOWERS Bright pink pom-pom-shaped flowers will appear on thin stems from midsummer to early autumn.

HARVEST Pick the flowers and leaves at the base of the stem and suspend upside down to dry in bunches or use them fresh. Snip the stems into tiny strips and break apart the flower heads to scatter over salads and soft cheeses. Stir into soups, stews and casseroles and combine with pizza and bread doughs. They have a strong onion-like flavour.

3 *ALOYSIA CITRODORA*
Lemon verbena

A shrub with edible flowers and foliage.

HEIGHT & SPREAD 1.5 × 1.5m (5 × 5ft)

GROWING Grow from small plants purchased at a nursery or garden centre. Lemon verbena makes a wonderful edging plant. It thrives in poor, stony soil and requires little water but should be positioned in full sun.

CARE Plants can be trimmed back in the autumn to keep them small and bushy. Propagate by taking woody cuttings.

FLOWERS Small clusters of tiny star-shaped white- or lilac-coloured flowers will appear in midsummer.

HARVEST Both the flowers and foliage have a strong lemony flavour. Harvest them at the same time to make tisanes or to perfume green or black tea leaves. Add to poached fruits, sorbets and ice creams or float in cocktails. Use to make syrups or floral sugars in cake and cookie recipes.

4 *ANGELICA OFFICINALIS*
Angelica, angel's fishing rod

A biennial with edible flowers, stems and foliage.

HEIGHT & SPREAD 2 × 1.2m (7 × 4ft)

GROWING Grow from seed scattered directly where you want it. Seedlings do not like to be transplanted. Sow the seed on the surface of the soil as they need light to germinate. Position at the back of the border or in a container. Angelicas are very striking architectural plants that grow to an unexpected height. They like to be in a shady position.

CARE Angelicas will self-seed but to be on the safe side, save your own for resowing.

FLOWERS As a biennial the flowers will only appear in the second season after seed sowing. In the first season you will see a mass of green foliage. The next year tall spires with rounded umbels of yellow flowers will put on a wonderful show in early summer.

HARVEST Pick the leaves and stems in the first year to use as a sweetener in poached fruits. Chop into small pieces to make botanical spirits by adding to unflavoured gin or vodka. When the flowers are ready, gently cut the umbels apart and crystallize the individual florets or scatter raw over cakes and desserts. All parts have a sweet taste and can be used in lieu of sugar.

5 *ANTHEMIS NOBILIS*
Common chamomile

A hardy perennial with edible flowers and foliage.

HEIGHT & SPREAD 30 × 30cm (12 × 12in)

GROWING Grow from seed where you want it to appear. Sow in the autumn or late spring. Seedlings will germinate quickly and go on to form a mat. Chamomile is good for speedy ground cover and looks wonderful in wildflower gardens. It will thrive in any soil and any position.

CARE Very little maintenance is required. Dig up pockets to replant elsewhere if it is spreading too quickly.

FLOWERS Tiny daisy-like flowers will appear throughout the summer. Both the flowers and foliage are highly aromatic and are a magnet for pollinating insects.

HARVEST Pick the flowers once they are fully out at the base of the stem and include foliage. Dry in suspended bunches and store in an airtight tin. Chamomile is commonly used for making tisanes. Both leaves and flowers have a honey-like flavour with reputed sleep-inducing properties. Drink the tea neat or use it for poaching fresh fruits or soaking dried fruits.

6 *ANTHRISCUS CEREFOLIUM*
Chervil

A hardy annual with edible flowers and foliage.

HEIGHT & SPREAD 50 × 50cm (20 × 20in)

GROWING Sow from seed where you want it to grow. If you sow successionally every few weeks in late spring, you will have plants throughout the year.

CARE Make sure the plants do not dry out completely. Roots should be kept moist.

FLOWERS Tiny clusters of white flowers will appear above sprays of attractive fern-like foliage all summer and into the autumn.

HARVEST Pick the flowers and foliage at the base of the stem and hang up in bunches to dry. Alternatively, use fresh in soups, stews and casseroles. Steep the flowers in oils and vinegars or blend into butters and soft cheeses. Combine in pizza and bread doughs. They have a light aniseed flavour.

7 *ARTEMISIA DRACUNCULUS*
Tarragon

A hardy perennial with edible flowers and foliage.

HEIGHT & SPREAD 50 × 50cm (20 × 20in)

GROWING Grow from seed sown in autumn or early spring. Once germination has taken place, thin out seedlings to 10cm (4in). Plants will put on rapid bushy growth. They should be in full sun and require good drainage.

CARE Pinch out the top green tips to encourage growth further down the stem. Cut back to ground level in late autumn or early winter for strong new shoots the following year.

FLOWERS Tiny yellow flowers appear on the thin pointed leaves of tarragon in late summer. Both leaves and flowers are highly aromatic and prized for their intense savoury flavour.

HARVEST Cut the flowers and foliage at the base of the stem and dry upside down in bunches or use fresh in salads and vegetable dishes. Tarragon pairs particularly well with tomatoes. Blend into soft cheeses or add to omelettes and other egg-based dishes.

8 *BORAGO OFFICINALIS*
Borage

A hardy annual with edible flowers.

HEIGHT & SPREAD 60 × 50cm (24 × 20in)

GROWING Grow from seed sown directly into the ground in autumn or early spring. Borage needs to be in full sun but will thrive in poor stony soil. It looks lovely as part of a wildflower planting scheme and is a magnet for bees and other useful pollinators.

CARE Save your own seed at the end of the flowering season to resow the following year.

FLOWERS Bright blue or white flowers will appear from midsummer onwards. The stems and leaves of borage tend to be quite prickly so wear gloves when handling the plants.

HARVEST Pick the flowers off the stems with a sharp pair of scissors. All parts of the flower are edible and the blue ones in particular look stunning used as a garnish or frozen in ice cubes. They taste like cucumber.

9 *CICHORIUM INTYBUS*
Chicory

A hardy perennial with edible flowers, foliage and roots.

HEIGHT & SPREAD 90 × 60cm (36 × 24in)

GROWING Grow from seed sown under cover in the autumn. Transplant seedlings to their growing position in the spring. Chicory requires a position in full sun to flower.

CARE Only minimal watering is needed. Do not allow roots to become waterlogged.

FLOWERS Delicate sky-blue flowers with an open daisy shape appear dotted along branching stems during the summer. They open and shut with the sun.

HARVEST Pick the flowers individually off the stems. Do not pick the actual stem if you want more flowers to come. They can be pickled or frozen in ice cubes. The roots of chicory have traditionally been ground and used as a coffee substitute. The leaves can be eaten as a salad. The whole plant has a slightly bitter taste.

10 *CORIANDRUM SATIVUM*
Coriander

A hardy annual with edible flowers, foliage and seeds.

HEIGHT & SPREAD 50 × 20cm (20 × 8in)

GROWING Grow from seed sown directly in autumn or spring. Thin out seedlings to 10cm (4in). For flowers, coriander should be positioned in full sun but it will produce plenty of foliage if grown in partial shade. You can also sow seed directly into pots for the kitchen windowsill.

CARE Allow some flowers to set seed for saving to sow the following year. The seeds are also edible.

FLOWERS Fragile-looking umbels of white and pink-purple flowers will appear in midsummer on thin wispy stems. Plants will start producing feathery foliage from late spring until early autumn.

HARVEST Pick the flowers and foliage to hang up in bunches to dry. Alternatively use fresh in all manner of savoury dishes. Coriander is delicious in stir-fries and curries and when added sparingly to soups and stews. The flowers can be steeped to flavour vinegars and oils and used to make herbal salt. They have a strong distinctive flavour with citrusy undertones.

11 *FILIPENDULA ULMARIA*
Meadowsweet

A hardy perennial with edible flowers and foliage.

HEIGHT & SPREAD 50 × 50cm (20 × 20in)

GROWING Grow from seed sown into containers in early spring. Transplant seedlings into the ground when they are big enough to handle. Meadowsweet is a wonderful addition to a wildflower garden or naturalistic planting scheme.

CARE Plants will gradually form clumps that can be lifted and divided in the autumn.

FLOWERS Creamy white clusters of perfumed flowers appear in midsummer. Foliage starts to appear from late spring through until the autumn. The whole plant will die back in the winter and appear again the following year.

HARVEST Pick the flowers as they arrive along with the foliage. Steep in alcohol or use to make sugar syrups and floral sugars for cake and pancake batters, desserts and puddings. They have a light caramel flavour with hints of vanilla.

12 *FOENICULUM VULGARE*
Common fennel

A hardy perennial with edible flowers, foliage and seeds (see page 45).

HEIGHT & SPREAD 1.5m × 45cm (5ft × 18in)

GROWING Grow from seed sown where you want it in autumn or spring. Seedlings do not like to be transplanted. Thin out newly germinated plants to a space of 50cm (20in). Fennel likes to be in full sun and will thrive in poor stony soil. Plant against a fence or a wall to create a structural backdrop for other plants.

CARE Minimal care is required. Fennel is very drought tolerant and needs little watering.

FLOWERS Airy flat-topped flowers made up of tiny individual florets in hues of bright yellow appear above stems of feathery foliage from mid- to late summer. They are a perfect landing pad for bees and other insects.

HARVEST Cut off the flowers and foliage at the base of the stem and suspend in bunches to dry for use throughout the winter. Use fresh in all manner of savoury dishes. Allow some flowers to set seed and save this for edible purposes too. Every part of the plant has a light liquorice flavour.

13 *LEVISTICUM OFFICINALE*
Lovage

A hardy perennial with edible flowers, stalks, foliage and roots.

HEIGHT & SPREAD 100 × 50cm (39 × 20in)

GROWING Grow from seed sown directly in the spring. Lovage requires full sun and space to spread out its roots. You could grow one plant in a large container. Position towards the back of a border.

CARE Do not allow the roots to dry out. Cut back to the ground in the autumn after flowering has finished. It will reappear the following year.

FLOWERS Green-yellow umbels appear in midsummer above the feathery fern-like foliage.

HARVEST Pick flowers and foliage at the base of stem and suspend for drying. Use fresh for a strong celery-like flavour in soups and stews. Chop finely to add to salts and steep in oils and vinegars. Scatter over soft cheese or combine into butter.

14 *MELISSA OFFICINALIS*
Lemon balm

A hardy perennial with edible flowers and foliage.

HEIGHT & SPREAD 50 × 50cm (20 × 20in)

GROWING Grow from seed sown in the spring where you want it to appear. Lemon balm forms a bushy clump and makes a lovely summer edging plant. It will thrive in partial shade.

CARE Little maintenance is required. Cut down to the ground in autumn and it will reappear the following year. Divide by the roots if plants start to become too big.

FLOWERS Delicate creamy-white flowers appear in midsummer above the bushy foliage, which looks like mint but smells distinctly of lemon.

HARVEST All parts of the plant have a strong citrus flavour and scent. Use in place of lemons in any type of dish. The flowers can be crystallized or floated in drinks. Blend the foliage with olive oil and garlic for a delicious pesto alternative. Steep in hot water to make a tisane or layer with green or black tea leaves.

15 *MENTHA SPICATA*
Spearmint

A hardy perennial with edible flowers and foliage.

HEIGHT & SPREAD 50 × 90cm (20 × 36in)

GROWING Grow from seed sown in the autumn or early spring. Spearmint has a suckering habit and spreads very rapidly. If you want to restrict its growth, then contain it in a pot. It will thrive in any position. You can happily keep it on a windowsill.

CARE Little maintenance is required. It can be divided very easily to make new plants in the autumn. Cut back to the ground to encourage new growth the following year.

FLOWERS Tall purple flower spikes will appear on bushy clumps of foliage in midsummer. Both the leaves and flowers have a distinctly recognizable refreshing scent. The flowers are very attractive to pollinating insects.

HARVEST Pick the flowers and foliage at the base of the stem and suspend in bunches to dry for use throughout the winter. Use fresh as a flavouring in all kinds of sweet and savoury dishes. The flowers can be eaten whole as a garnish or crystallized. Use flowers and foliage to make sugars and syrups and cordials, sorbets and ice creams or steep in hot water to make a soothing tea.

16 MYRRHIS ODORATA
Sweet cicely

A hardy perennial with edible flowers, foliage and seeds.

HEIGHT & SPREAD 100 × 50cm (39 × 20in)

GROWING Grow from seed sown in the autumn or spring where you want it to appear. Sweet cicely will thrive in shade – it grows tall so position it towards the back of a border.

CARE Little maintenance is required. Divide by the roots in autumn.

FLOWERS Large clusters of creamy-white flowers appear above the ferny foliage in midsummer. They resemble elderflowers in appearance. They are highly fragrant and are very attractive to pollinating insects.

HARVEST Both the flowers and foliage are very sweet in flavour and can be used as a sugar substitute. Add to sour poached fruits or use to make cordials and syrups. Whole flower heads can be coated in batter and lightly fried.

17 OCIMUM BASILICUM
Sweet basil

A half-hardy annual with edible flowers and foliage.

HEIGHT & SPREAD 40 × 40cm (16 × 16in)

GROWING Grow from seed sown under cover in late spring. Basil is a perfect pot plant and will sit very happily on a windowsill. If you are growing it outside, position in full sun. It requires warmth to put on growth.

CARE Pinch out fresh green tips to encourage growth further down the stem. Water sparingly.

FLOWERS Small white or pink-purple flowers appear in midsummer. Foliage will arrive first and the plant will continue to put on growth once the flowers have finished.

HARVEST Both the leaves and flowers are highly aromatic with a distinctive fresh perfume. Pick with abundance and blitz with pine nuts, olive oil and garlic to make your own fresh pesto. Scatter on to pizza doughs and breads. Combine with tomatoes and other fresh vegetables for salads.

18 OREGANO VULGARE
Majoram

A hardy perennial with edible flowers and leaves.

HEIGHT & SPREAD 50 × 50cm (20 × 20in)

GROWING Grow from seed sown directly into the ground in early spring. Oregano is happy in shade and will thrive in poor stony soil. It will put on growth to form small clumps.

CARE No real maintenance is required. Cut back old stems and divide plants by the roots in autumn if they become too big.

FLOWERS Pretty clusters of pink-purple flowers will appear in midsummer and throughout the autumn. They are particularly attractive to bees and other insects.

HARVEST Cut the flower stems and foliage away from the base of the plant. Suspend in bunches to dry for use throughout the winter. Both the leaves and flowers have a strong savoury flavour. Use fresh to roll into pasta, scatter over bread and pizza doughs, combine with soft cheeses, stir into soups and make herbal salts.

19 PETROSELINUM CRISPUM
Curly parsley

A hardy annual with edible flowers and foliage.

HEIGHT & SPREAD 40 × 40cm (16 × 16in)

GROWING Grow from seed sown directly where you want it to appear. Parsley is perfect for pots on the windowsill. It is happy in any position.

CARE No special care is required. If growing in a pot, do not let the roots dry out.

FLOWERS Curly parsley is traditionally grown for its aromatic foliage. The flowers tend to take second place but in midsummer small umbels of white flowers will appear above the leaves. They are less flavoursome but can be used for edible purposes where only a hint of parsley is required.

HARVEST Pick the leaves and flowers as needed. Use the leaves on salads and in soups and stews. The flowers can be steeped in oils and vinegars or chopped finely with leaves to make herbal salts.

20 SALVIA OFFICINALIS
Common sage

An evergreen shrub with edible flowers and foliage.

HEIGHT & SPREAD 50 × 50cm (20 × 20in)

GROWING Purchase as a small plant from a nursery or garden centre. Sage is happy in any position and will thrive in partial shade. Plant towards the back of the border. You can also grow it in a container.

CARE Prune back lightly in spring so it keeps its shape.

FLOWERS Blue-purple flower spikes will appear in the summer above the attractive grey-green foliage. Sage has a distinctive slightly medicinal aroma.

HARVEST Pick the flowers from the base of the stem and suspend in bunches to dry. Use fresh as a flavouring for all types of savoury dishes. Steep leaves and flowers in hot water to make tea – known as 'thinkers' tea' – sage is thought to boost concentration.

㉑ *SALVIA ROSMARINUS*
Rosemary

An evergreen shrub with edible flowers and foliage.

HEIGHT & SPREAD 1.5 × 1.5m (5 × 5ft)

GROWING Grow from small plants purchased from a nursery or garden centre. Plant in full sun in well-drained soil. Rosemary plants make fantastic informal hedging if allowed to grow to their full height.

CARE Prune lightly in spring if you want to restrict the height and spread.

FLOWERS A show of tiny blue-mauve flowers will appear in spring and summer. As an evergreen, foliage is on display all year round. Both flowers and foliage are highly aromatic with a distinctive slightly astringent perfume.

HARVEST Pick bunches when the flowers are in bloom. Cut at the base of the stem to include foliage and suspend upside down to dry. Use fresh in fish and meat dishes and as a flavouring for alcohol and waters. Make syrups and sugars for use in sorbets and ice creams. Rosemary works well in both sweet and savoury foods.

㉒ *SALVIA VIRIDIS*
Clary sage, painted sage

A hardy annual with edible flowers, bracts and foliage.

HEIGHT & SPREAD 50 × 50cm (20 × 20in)

GROWING Grow from seed where you want it to appear sown in autumn or spring. Thin out seedlings after germination. Clary sage can easily be grown in pots for the windowsill. It requires a sunny position.

CARE Little maintenance is required. Allow some flowers to set seed to save for resowing.

FLOWERS Colourful flowers in pinks, mauves and deep blues will appear throughout the summer. They grow on equally colourful bracts.

HARVEST Pick flowers on the bracts and suspend in bunches to dry. Use flowers and leaves fresh in salads and vegetable dishes. They add beautiful pops of colour. Their taste is similar to regular sage with an undertone of mint.

23 *SINAPIS ALBA*
White mustard

A hardy annual with edible flowers and foliage.

HEIGHT & SPREAD 60 × 40cm (24 × 16in)

GROWING Grow from seed scattered where you want it to appear. Germination is rapid. Thin out seedlings as necessary. Mustard plants look wonderful as part of a wildflower scheme and are very attractive to pollinating insects.

CARE No special care is required. Although it will self-seed naturally, allow some flowers to set seed for resowing the following year.

FLOWERS Despite its name, the flowers of white mustard are bright yellow. Small clusters will appear on the plant throughout the summer.

HARVEST Pick flowers and foliage at the base of the stem and separate before use. The leaves are delicious as a salad or when steamed and dressed with olive oil. Scatter the flowers over the tops of salads and other vegetable dishes. Both flowers and foliage are slightly peppery in taste.

24 *THYMUS VULGARIS*
Thyme

A hardy perennial with edible flowers and foliage.

HEIGHT & SPREAD Up to 30 × 30cm (12 × 12in)

GROWING Grow from seed sown into a tray or pots under cover. Transplant seedlings when they are big enough to handle and plant in a sunny position or keep in pots on the windowsill.

CARE Do not overwater. Thyme is extremely drought tolerant and hates to have its roots permanently wet.

FLOWERS Throughout the summer tiny pink, purple and white flowers will appear on mounds of small green leaves. Both are extremely aromatic and attractive to insects.

HARVEST Cut flowers and foliage at the base of the stems. They will be too short to suspend so lay them out on a tray to dry naturally for use throughout the winter. Use fresh in soups and stews. Make syrups, sugars and salts. The flavour can be harnessed for both sweet and savoury dishes.

25 *VALERIANA OFFICINALIS*
Common valerian

A hardy perennial with edible flowers, leaves and roots.

HEIGHT & SPREAD 1.5m × 40cm (5ft × 16in)

GROWING Grow from seed sown under cover in spring. Transplant when plants are big enough to handle. Plant against a fence or wall or at the back of the border. It will thrive in partial shade. Valerian is tall and thin and also looks good as part of a wildflower scheme towering above smaller flowers.

CARE Allow some flowers to set seed to resow for the following year. Do not cut back until spring – the seed heads are a good food source for birds in winter. If new seedlings become invasive then remove them.

FLOWERS White or pink florets will appear throughout the summer. They have a delicate sweet perfume.

HARVEST Pick flowers and foliage at the base of the stem and suspend in bunches for drying. Use the leaves fresh to make tisanes – they are thought to help sleep. The flowers can be crystallized for decorating cakes.

Vegetable flowers

❶ *ALLIUM CEPA*
Onion

An annual bulb with edible flowers and foliage.

HEIGHT & SPREAD 50 × 10cm (20 × 4in)

GROWING Grow from untreated sets planted in spring for edible flowers. Space out in a row at 10cm (4in) apart and plant so the nose pokes out of the soil. Position in full sun in well-drained soil.

CARE Do not allow bulbs to sit in water. Improve the soil with plenty of organic matter before planting.

FLOWERS You will need to allow your bulbs to bolt and produce a flower stalk. For normal onion growing the flower stalk would be removed. A spherical white flower made of tiny individual florets will form on each stalk.

HARVEST Cut off the flower at the base of the stem. Suspend upside-down for drying to use throughout the winter or cut off individual florets to use fresh for flavouring breads, salads, pizza doughs, pasta and rice dishes.

❷ *ALLIUM SATIVUM*
Garlic

A perennial bulb with edible flowers and foliage.

HEIGHT & SPREAD 50 × 10cm (20 × 4in)

GROWING Grow from bulbs and choose hardneck varieties for edible flowers. Garlic requires a position in full sun in well-drained soil. It is easy to grow in pots.

CARE Little maintenance is required. Do not allow pot-grown plants to dry out.

FLOWERS Umbels of pink-white flowers will appear in midsummer on leafless stalks amongst thin straps of foliage. Both flowers and foliage have a distinct smell of garlic.

HARVEST Pick the flowers at the base of the stem and suspend upside-down in bunches for drying or use fresh. Snip off the individual florets from the flower head to scatter over all types of savoury dishes or cook in stir-fries, soups and stews in place of garlic bulbs.

❸ *APIUM GRAVEOLENS*
Celery

A half-hardy annual with edible flowers and foliage.

HEIGHT & SPREAD 50 × 50cm (20 × 20in)

GROWING Grow from seed sown where you want it in spring. For regular picking sow seed successively over a couple of weeks. Celery prefers to be in full sun but will tolerate partial shade.

CARE No special maintenance is required.

FLOWERS Tiny sprigs of green-white flowers will appear in midsummer amongst the fern-like foliage. Both flowers and leaves taste of celery.

HARVEST Snip off the flowers as they appear. Use to flavour oils or chop finely with a few leaves to make salts. Scatter over salads or soft cheeses, combine into yoghurt for a savoury dip or roll into pasta dough.

4 *CUCUMIS SATIVUS*
Cucumber

A half-hardy annual with edible flowers and fruits.

HEIGHT & SPREAD 1.5m × 60cm (5ft × 24in)

GROWING Grow from seeds sown in pots in spring. Keep under cover until plants are large enough to handle and any danger of frost has passed. Transplant to larger containers. Cucumbers prefer moist humid conditions. They are perfect greenhouse plants.

CARE Plants will need support in the form of canes and string to grow upwards.

FLOWERS Cucumber flowers are male and female. Only the female flowers produce fruit and will appear as the fruits begin to swell. Both types of flowers are edible and are bright yellow in colour. They only appear for one day before dropping off.

HARVEST Pick the flowers as they open and store in the fridge. Coat in batter and cook in oil or use fresh as a garnish for salads or other vegetable dishes. Preserve them by pickling in brine – they will lose their colour but retain their flavour.

5 *CUCURBITA PEPO*
Courgette

A half-hardy annual with edible flowers and fruits.

HEIGHT & SPREAD
50cm × 100cm (20 × 39in)

GROWING Grow from seed planted in spring in pots kept under cover in a warm sunny position until germination takes place. Transplant to a larger container when seedlings are large enough to handle and keep protected until the first frosts have passed before planting outside.

CARE Water well in dry spells.

FLOWERS Like cucumbers, bright yellow courgette flowers are male and female. Female flowers develop with the fruit. Male flowers drop away once pollination is complete. Both are edible.

HARVEST Use as close to possible from the picking time if you do not want them to close up. They can be stored in the fridge. Coat in batter and deep fry or stuff with soft herby cheese and bake in the oven. Separate the flowers to scatter petals over salads and cold vegetable dishes.

6 *ERUCA VESICARIA*
Rocket

A half-hardy annual with edible flowers and leaves.

HEIGHT & SPREAD 30 × 30cm (12 × 12in)

GROWING Grow from seed sown where you want it in spring. Thin out seedlings after germination. Rocket prefers a sunny spot but will tolerate partial shade.

CARE Rocket is a cut-and-come-again plant. The more you pick the more it grows.

FLOWERS In order to produce flowers you need to allow the plant to bolt and develop a flower stalk. Do not remove it. Pretty white flowers with purple veins and yellow stamens will appear throughout the summer.

HARVEST Pick the flowers away from the stem. Use to flavour all types of savoury dishes. Rocket has a strong peppery taste. The leaves make a delicious salad. Dress with olive oil and scatter the flowers over the top.

7 *PHASEOLUS COCCINEUS*
Runner bean

A half-hardy annual with edible flowers and pods.

HEIGHT & SPREAD 4m × 50cm (13ft × 20in)

GROWING Grow from seed sown in the spring directly where you want your beans. Choose dwarf varieties for growing in pots if space is limited. Runner beans like to be in full sun in well-drained fertile soil.

CARE Runner beans grow on vines that need support in the form of a trellis or wigwam made from canes.

FLOWERS Clusters of bright scarlet flowers will appear before the pods form throughout the summer months.

HARVEST Pick the flowers as they appear and store in the fridge. They have a bean-like taste and can be used in omelettes, frittatas and other egg-based dishes, scattered over salads or cooked in soups and stews.

8 *PISUM SATIVUM*
Garden pea

A half-hardy annual with edible flowers, pods and shoots.

NOTE *Do not eat the flowers or any other parts of* Lathyrus odoratus *(ornamental sweet peas).*

HEIGHT & SPREAD 60 × 30cm (24 × 12in)

GROWING Grow from seed sown into drills or rows in late spring. Pea plants require full sun. Sow successively over a couple of weeks to extend the harvesting period.

CARE Peas use their own tendrils to cling on to a support and climb upwards. Use twiggy hazel sticks or bamboo canes for this purpose.

FLOWERS Pink, purple or white flowers will appear in early summer and develop into pods. Do not pick all the flowers if you want to harvest pods.

HARVEST Snip off the flowers and young shoots to add to salads and for scattering over stir-fries and cold soups. Combine into soft cheeses or thick yoghurt for a pea-flavoured dip.

9 *TRAGOPOGON PORRIFOLIUS*
Salsify

A hardy perennial with edible petals and roots.

HEIGHT & SPREAD 50 × 50cm (20 × 20in)

GROWING Grow from seed sown directly where you want it in a sunny spot. Thin out after germination to leave the strongest looking seedlings in place.

CARE Little maintenance is required.

FLOWERS Large pink flowers that resemble dandelions will appear above the grass-like foliage throughout the summer. The flowers open in the morning and shut again in the evening.

HARVEST Pick the flowers as they are open and gently remove the petals to scatter over all types of savoury dishes. To harvest the parsnip-like roots you will need to dig up the whole plant. They can be roasted or boiled.

10 *VICA FABA*
Broad bean

A hardy annual with edible flowers and pods.

HEIGHT & SPREAD 100 × 30cm (39 × 12in)

GROWING Grow from seeds planted where you want them – the seeds are large enough to be spaced out evenly at around 20cm (8in) in rows or choose dwarf varieties for containers if space is limited.

CARE Broad beans will need staking to provide support and allow them to grow upwards.

FLOWERS Flowers will appear before the pods in a range of beautiful pink and purple colours. Look for heritage varieties for the most sumptuous hues.

HARVEST Snip off the flowers from the main stem and store in the fridge. Use as a garnish for salads and vegetable dishes, or add to stir-fries, soups and stews. They have a delicate bean flavour.

Flower foliage

① *ACHILLEA*
Yarrow

A hardy perennial with edible leaves.

HEIGHT & SPREAD 90 × 60cm (36 × 24in)

GROWING Grow from seed sown directly in the autumn or spring where you want the plants to appear or as small plug plants. Achilleas like a sunny spot and look good as part of a naturalistic planting scheme.

CARE They are extremely drought tolerant and do not like to sit with their roots in water. Divide plants in the autumn when you see new babies appearing at the side of the parent.

FOLIAGE Layers of aromatic feathery green foliage appear under the flat plate-shaped flowers throughout the summer.

HARVEST Pick leaves when they are young and tender as the flowers are in bloom. You can also eat the tiny flower florets, but the main flavour is in the foliage, which has a taste of aniseed. Treat them as a vegetable – steam or boil them and dress with olive oil or butter before serving. Add to soups and sauces or serve raw as part of a green salad.

② *CYCLAMEN PERSICUM*
Persian cyclamen

A half-hardy tuber with edible leaves.

HEIGHT & SPREAD 20 × 20cm (8 × 8in)

GROWING Grow from tubers planted in early autumn or late spring. They are best grown in pots and containers, and although they flower in early winter they will die back after flowering and will not withstand frosts. They can be grown indoors as house plants.

CARE Water sparingly and remove any yellow leaves and spent flower heads with a sharp pair of scissors.

FOLIAGE Pretty heart-shaped marbled leaves will continue to appear throughout late autumn and early winter. If you are growing them indoors you can keep them going for much longer.

HARVEST Pick the leaves and use them in the same way as vine leaves to fill with rice or other grains. Roll them tightly and bake in the oven.

③ *MYRTUS COMMUNIS*
Myrtle

A hardy evergreen shrub with edible leaves.

HEIGHT & SPREAD 3 × 3m (10 × 10ft)

GROWING Grow from small plants purchased at a nursery or garden centre. Myrtle makes a wonderful hedge and is an alternative to box. It requires a sunny position away from direct winds.

CARE Cut back in late spring to encourage fresh new leaves. As a hedging plant you can keep it to one height by shearing the top growth.

FOLIAGE Glossy dark green diamond-shaped leaves are on permanent show. When you brush against them they give off a deliciously aromatic perfume.

HARVEST Pick the new young leaves to steep in oils and alcohol. Combine with flowers to make jams and infuse in honey. Add to soups, stews and casseroles. Myrtle leaves are astringent in taste, contain anti-inflammatory properties and are rich in vitamin C. You can also use them to make tisanes or to flavour green or black tea leaves.

4 PELARGONIUM
Storksbill

A tender perennial with edible leaves (see page 61).

HEIGHT & SPREAD 40 × 30cm (16 × 12in)

GROWING Purchase as small plants from a nursery, garden centre or specialist grower. Pelargoniums require full sun and as tender perennials will not tolerate frost. Grow them in pots to bring indoors during the colder months.

CARE They will go into a period of dormancy over the winter. Cut back the leaves and reserve for cooking or freezing. Water no more than once a week during this time. In spring when they go back outside they will put on plenty of fresh new growth.

FOLIAGE Choose any variety of scented pelargonium to grow specifically for perfume and flavouring food. The leaves remain green all year round.

HARVEST Leaves can be picked at any point in the growing cycle. Use them to make floral sugars and syrups to add to cake and cookie batters. Chop them to add to fruit salads or combine with poached fruits. Their flavours, particularly 'Attar of Roses', pair well with chocolate.

5 SANTOLINA CHAMNECYPARISSUS
Cotton lavender

A hardy evergreen shrub with edible leaves.

HEIGHT & SPREAD 90 × 50cm (36 × 20in)

GROWING Purchase as a small plant from a nursery or garden centre. Cotton lavenders make good edging plants in formal schemes but also look lovely in gravel gardens. They are extremely drought tolerant, will thrive in poor stony soil but require full sun.

CARE They require little maintenance but can be cut back in the autumn so they keep their shape.

FOLIAGE Dense feathery leaves that change from a verdant green to a silvery grey over time are on constant display. They are highly scented with an aromatic perfume that is released when they are picked.

HARVEST Dry bunches of cotton lavender suspended upside down for year-round use in the kitchen. The leaves have an olive-like flavour and can be used in soups, stews, sauces and marinades or combine them into bread and pizza doughs.

Flower seeds

① ANETHUM GRAVEOLENS
Dill

A hardy annual with edible flowers, foliage and seeds.

HEIGHT & SPREAD 100 × 50cm (39 × 20in)

GROWING Grow from seed sown in the autumn or spring directly where you want it to appear, ideally in a sunny spot at the back of a border. Thin out after germination but do not transplant seedlings as they hate to be moved. Sow a couple of seeds in a large container if space is limited.

CARE No special maintenance is required.

FLOWERS/SEEDS Umbels of bright yellow flowers will appear throughout the summer above the feathery fern-like foliage. Allow the flowers to set seed in the autumn. All parts of the plant have a mild aniseed flavour.

HARVEST Gather the seed by snipping off the ripe heads into a paper bag. As they dry out they will detach themselves from the head – shaking the bag will encourage this. Store the tiny oval grey-brown seeds in a jam jar. Use in pickles, marinades and dressings or scatter over bread and pastry doughs.

② CARUM CARVI
Caraway

A hardy biennial with edible foliage and seeds.

HEIGHT & SPREAD 100 × 50cm (39 × 20in)

GROWING Grow from seed sown in spring directly where you want it to appear. Thin out seedlings but do not transplant. Choose a sunny spot and sow into well-drained soil.

CARE Do not allow the roots to sit in water.

FLOWERS/SEEDS Delicate pink or white flowers made up of many individual florets will appear in midsummer in the second year of growth. The tiny brown crescent-shaped seeds will ripen a month after flowering. Both flowers and foliage are highly aromatic, and the seeds have a distinctive flavour of rye.

HARVEST Gather the seed and store in a spice jar or jam jar. Use to scatter over soft cheeses, in sauerkraut or other cabbage-based dishes, breads and pastry doughs and caraway seed cake.

3 *LINUM*
Flax, linseed

A hardy perennial with edible seeds.

HEIGHT & SPREAD 50 × 50cm (20 × 20in)

GROWING Grow from seed in autumn or early spring, scattered liberally where you want it to grow. Flax likes a sunny spot and is a beautiful addition to a wildflower meadow. It is happy in poor, stony soil. Sow successively for a regular harvest.

CARE There is no requirement to water. Flax prefers very dry conditions and is extremely drought tolerant.

FLOWERS/SEEDS Bright blue saucer-shaped flowers will appear briefly on each plant throughout the summer. They rapidly form seed pods the size of a pea. Each one is filled with about ten seeds.

HARVEST Allow the pods to ripen on the plant. Release the seeds by gently crushing each pod. Store the tiny golden-brown seeds in a spice jar and add to granolas and other cereal-based dishes or sprinkle into soups and stews. Linseed is an excellent source of omega 3.

4 *NIGELLA SATIVA*
Black cumin

A hardy annual with edible seeds.

HEIGHT & SPREAD 20 × 10cm (8 × 4in)

GROWING Grow from seed sown directly where you want it to appear in the autumn. Thin out seedlings to 10cm (4in). *Nigella sativa* is closely related to the more commonly grown ornamental *Nigella damascena* and looks wonderful as part of a wildflower scheme. It will thrive in stony soil and tolerates partial shade.

CARE No special maintenance is required.

FLOWERS/SEEDS Delicate flowers in blue or white will appear in early to midsummer. They will go on to form beautiful seed pods that resemble tiny balloons. Each one is divided into several capsules filled with tiny black pip-shaped seeds.

HARVEST Once the seed pods are ripe, cut them off the plant and gently crush to release the seed. Store in an airtight jar. They have a mild taste of toasted onions and can be used as a flavour replacement in bread and pastry doughs, rice or egg-based dishes, soups and stews.

5 *PAPAVER SOMNIFERUM*
Opium poppy

A hardy annual with edible seeds.

HEIGHT & SPREAD 90 × 50cm (36 × 20in)

GROWING Grow from seed scattered where you want it to appear in the autumn or early spring. Opium poppies will tolerate partial shade and poor soil. They are extremely drought resistant. Thin out seedlings once germination has taken place.

CARE No special maintenance is required.

FLOWERS/SEEDS Exotic-looking multi-petalled flower heads will appear from early summer in deep rich shades depending on the variety. The flowers are short-lived and as the petals fall away they will reveal a large bulbous seed pod with a flat indented top that will gradually turn from green to brown as it matures.

HARVEST The seeds are ripe when the pod rattles as it is shaken. Cut off from the main stem and gently shake out the seed on to a cloth. Gather and store in an airtight jar. Poppy seeds have a nutty flavour and add crunch to cakes and muffins, granolas and other cereal-based dishes.

List of toxic plants

To ensure their survival some common garden plants have developed toxic compounds. These act as warning signals to predators and prevent them from being eaten. The following list of flowers and plants are toxic and should **not** be consumed under any circumstances. Ideally, flowers grown for eating should be at a distance from them.

- *Aconitum* (monkshood)
- *Agapanthus* (African lily)
- *Agrostemma githago* (corncockle)
- *Alstromeira* (Peruvian lily)
- *Brugmansia* (angel's trumpet)
- *Colchium autumnale* (autumn crocus)
- *Convallaria majalis* (lily-of-the-valley)
- *Delphinium* (larkspur)
- *Digitalis* (foxglove)
- *Euphorbia* (spurge)
- *Galanthus* (snowdrop)
- *Hyacinthoides* (bluebell)
- *Hydrangea* (hydrangea)
- *Ipomea* (morning glory)
- *Lathyrus odoratus* (sweet pea)
- *Lupinus* (lupin)
- *Narcissus* (daffodil)
- *Nicotiana* (tobacco plant)
- *Oleander* (oleander)
- *Ranunculus* (buttercup)
- *Rhododendron* (rhodendron)
- *Zantedeschia* (calla lily)

Useful resources

SEEDS UK
Chiltern Seeds: chilternseeds.co.uk
Higgledy Garden: higgledygarden.com
Sarah Raven: sarahraven.com
Alma Proust: almaproust.com
Thompson & Morgan: thompson-morgan.com
Pennards Plants (heritage seeds):
pennardplants.com

SEEDS US
Floret: floretflowers.com

PLANTS (GENERAL)
Crocus: crocus.co.uk
Sarah Raven: sarahraven.com
RHS nursery finder: rhs.org.uk

BULBS
Peter Nyssen: peternyssen.com
Farmer Gracy: farmergracy.co.uk

ROSES
David Austin Roses: davidaustinroses.com

DIANTHUS AND CARNATIONS
Calamazag Plant Nursery:
calamazagnursery.co.uk
Whetman Garden Plants:
whetmangardenplants.co.uk

PELARGONIUMS
Woottens of Wenhaston: woottensplants.com

BIODEGRADABLE POTS
Wool Pots: woolpots.co.uk
Coir Pots: sarahraven.com

SOIL AND SOIL HEALTH
Peat free compost: dalefootcomposts.co.uk
Climate compost: thelandgardeners.com
Bio Char seed compost for propagation:
sarahraven.com

ORGANIC GARDENING TOURS AND COURSES AND FURTHER INFORMATION
Charles Dowding: charlesdowding.co.uk
Organic Garden: organicgarden.org.uk

WILDLIFE
Hedgehogs: britishhedgehogs.org.uk
Bumblebees: bumblebeeconservation.org
Butterflies: butterflyconservation.org

Index

lavender shortbread 58
macaroons 92
nasturtium trio 74, *75*
pellie loaf cake with pellie frosted
    topping 62, *63*
petal confetti cookies 86
pickled fennel flowers 46, *47*
rose pavlova 66, *67*
rustic sunflower breadsticks 70, *71*
seeded flatbreads 97
seeded muffins 91
shaved fennel salad 46, *47*
sorbet 95
sparkling floral jellies 83
sunflower bean dip 70, *71*
red clover (*trifolium pratense*) *140*, 141
rhizomes 31, 129, 142
risottos 38, 101, 102, 103
rocket (*eruca vesicaria*) 98, 101, 141, 156,
    156
roots 16, 27, 28, 32, 33
rose (*rosa*) 15, 32, 33, *64*, 65, 84, 138, *139*
    pavlova 66, *67*
    petals 66, 79, 84, 87, 88
    syrup 66, 79, 87
    water 66, 88
rose of Sharon (*Hibiscus syriacus*) *48*, 49,
    131, *131*
rosemary (*salvia rosmarinus*) 92, 152, *152*
Royal Horticultural Society (RHS) 33
runner bean (*phaseolus coccineus*) 156, *156*

S
sage (*salvia*) 28 *see also* baby sage,
    common sage, clary sage, painted sage
salads 15, 37, 102
salsify (*tragopogon porrifolius*) *156*, 157

salvia microphylla (baby sage) 139, *139*
salvia officinalis (common sage) 151, *151*
salvia rosmarinus (rosemary) 92, 152, *152*
salvia viridis (clary sage, painted sage) 152,
    152
sambucus (elderflower) 32, 79, 84, 98, 106,
    139, *139*
sambucus nigra (common elder) 139, *139*
santolina chamnecyparissus (cotton
    lavender) 159, *159*
savoury pastry dough bases 104
scrambled eggs 104
seasonal planting 30–31
seed sowing 24, 25, 26–7
seeded flatbreads 97
seedlings 26–7, 29
seeds 88, 96, 97, 130, 160–61
sepals 18, 19
shaved fennel salad 46
shortbread 58, 132, 133, 141
shrubs 12, 15, 32–3, 49, 122, 128, 139,
    140
sinapis alba (white mustard) 152, 153
snapdragon (*antirrhinum*) 102, 123, *123*
snowbell, three-cornered leek (*allium
    triquetum*) 122, *123*
society garlic (*tulbaghia violacea*) 142, *143*
softwood cuttings 28–9
soil
    acidic 125, 130
    bacteria 11
    healthy 11, 16
    poor 123, 132–6, 141, 161
    stony 141, 144, 145–6, 148, 150, 159,
        161
    well-drained 41, 49, 57, 122, 125,
        127–9, 131, 135, 152, 160

sorbet 95, 114

soups 100

sparkling floral jellies 83

spearmint (*mentha spicata*) *148*, 149

stamen 18, 19

sterilizing jars 80

stigma 12, 18, 19

stir fries 102

stock 101, 107

storksbill (*pelargonium*) 8, 28, 35, 60, 61, 62, 92, 93, 128, 159, *159*

style 18, 19

sulphur cosmos (*cosmos sulphureus*) 127, *127*

sunflower (*helianthus annuus*) 24, *68*, 69, 70, 86, 94, 96, 97, 114, 130, *131*

sunflower bean dip 70, *71*

sweet alyssum (*lobularia maritima*) *132*, 133

sweet basil (*ocimum basilicum*) 150, *151*

sweet cicely (*myrrhis odorata*) 92, 150, *151*

sweet violet (*viola odorata*) 79, 80, 143, *143*

sweet woodruff (*gallium odoratum*) 128, 129

syringa (lilac) 32, 79, 80, 82, 84, 92

syringa vulgaris (common lilac) 140, *140*

T

tagetes patula (French marigold) 96, 140, *140*

taraxacum officinale (dandelion) 12, 102, *140*, 141, 157

tarragon (*artemisia dracunculus*) 96, 146, *147*

tea plant (*camellia sinensis*) 125, *125*

teas and tisanes 88

tender perennials 28, 29

thyme (*thymus vulgaris*) 96, *152*, 153

toxic plants 164

tragopogon porrifolius (salsify) *156*, 157

trees 12, 15

trifolium pratense (red clover) *140*, 141

tropaeolum majus (nasturtium) 72, 73, 74, 75, *140*, 141

true leaves 26, 27

tubers 30–31

tulbaghia violacea (society garlic) 142, *143*

tulip (*tulipa*) 30, 31, 135, 142, *143*

U

unsweetened juices 88

V

valeriana officinalis (common valerian) *152*, 153

vegetable flowers 7, 98, 121, 154–7

vica faba (broad bean) 98, *156*, 157

vinegar 73, 98, 105, 118

viola (pansy) 98, 106, 118, 142, *143*

viola odorata (sweet violet) 79, 80, 143, *143*

vitamin C 15, 49, 158

W

watering 26, 32, 57, 61

weeds 12, 16, 124, 141

white mustard (*sinapis alba*) *152*, 153

wild fennel (*Foeniculum sativus*) 45

wisteria (*wisteria*) 33

worms 16, 32

Y

yarrow (*achillea*) 158, *159*

Z

zinnia (*zinnia*) 25, 86, 143, *143*

Acknowledgements

The making of a book is always much more than the work of one person. Many thanks to all the people who have been in involved in this project:

My publisher and the team at Pimpernel Press, especially Anna Sanderson; designer Sarah Pyke for her clear creative vision and grasp of the concept; Joanna Yee for her beautiful food images and for being so generous with her time and styling skills and the loan of all her wonderful props; Nick Hodgson for being on hand always with his camera for impromptu photography of our garden mainly at 6 o'clock in the morning; Sarah Cuttle for coming to photograph my garden on spec; my darling children Emily, Alice and Edward, who have been my main recipe testers over the years — this book is for you and I hope we will have many more communal meals as our family expands.

Photo credits

www.pimpernelpress.com

*A Floral Feast: A guide to growing and cooking with
edible flowers, foliage, herbs and seeds*

© Pimpernel Press Limited 2024
Text © Carolyn Dunster 2024
Photographs © see page 175

A catalogue record for this book is available from the British Library

Designed by Sarah Pyke
Typeset in Source Serif Pro and Jost

ISBN 978-1-914902-11-6

Printed and bound in China
9 8 7 6 5 4 3 2 1